OWENS VAL
RECEPTION CE
MANZANAR, CA
U.S. ENGINEER OF

LEONARD G. HOGUE   JOHN
AREA ENGINEER   RESID

OWENS   VALLEY
-CEPTION CENTER..
MANZANAR, CALIF.
J.S. ENGINEER OFFICE

|ARD G. HOGUE | JOHN H. HEINMILLER
A ENGINEER | RESIDENT ENGINEER

SUPREME COURT MILESTONES

Korematsu v. United States:

japanese-american internment

SUSAN   DUDLEY   GOLD

Marshall Cavendish
Benchmark
New York

Dedicated to Fred Toyosaburo Korematsu, Jan. 30, 1919–March 30, 2005, an American hero whose courage and persistence helped preserve the Bill of Rights for us all.

With special thanks to Professor David M. O'Brien of the Woodrow Wilson Department of Politics at the University of Virginia for reviewing the text of this book.

Marshall Cavendish Benchmark
99 White Plains Road
Tarrytown, NY 10591
www.marshallcavendish.us

All Internet sites were available and accurate when sent to press.

Library of Congress Cataloging-in-Publication Data · Gold, Susan Dudley. · *Korematsu v. United States* : Japanese-American internment / by Susan Dudley Gold.—1st ed. · p. cm.—(Supreme Court milestones) · Summary: "Describes the historical context of the Korematsu versus United States Supreme Court Case, detailing the claims made by both sides and the outcome, and including excerpts from the Supreme Court justices' decisions and relevant sidebars"—Provided by publisher. · Includes bibliographical references and index. · ISBN 0-7614-1943-8 · 1. Korematsu, Fred, 1919–Trials, litigation, etc. 2. United States—Trials, litigation, etc. 3. United States—Claims. 4. Japanese Americans—Evacuation and relocation, 1942–1945. I. Title: Korematsu versus United States. II. Title. III. Series. · KF228.K59G65 2005 · 342.7308'73—dc22 · 2005002534

Photo research by Candlepants Incorporated
The photographs in this book are used by permission and through the courtesy of: *Corbis*: Bettmann, 1, 2-3, 18, 21, 92, 115, 118; Museum of History & Industry, 33; 49, 50, 108; The Mariners Museum, 74. *Time Life Pictures/Getty Images*: 6, 56; *National Archives & Records Administration*: 12, 86, 121. *Seattle Times Company*: 57; *AP Wide World Photo*: 73; 124, 126. *White House Office of Record Management, Bush Presidential Records, George Bush Presidential Library #184767*. ME001: 123.

Series design by Sonia Chaghatzbanian
Printed in China · 1 3 5 6 4 2

contents

Carrying their possessions, the first of thousands of Japanese Americans arrive at Manzanar internment camp on March 21, 1942. Manzanar, the first of ten camps to open, served as both prison and home for Japanese-American detainees forced to leave their homes on the West Coast. The last of the detainees were permitted to leave in November 1945.

INTRODUCTION

A "LEGALIZATION OF RACISM"

Is it true, that the moment a declaration of war is made, the executive department of this government, without an act of Congress, becomes absolute master of our liberties and our lives? Are we, then, subject to martial rule, administered by the President upon his own sense of the exigency, with nobody to control him, and with every magistrate and every authority in the land subject to his will alone?

———Attorney David Dudley Field in *Ex parte Milligan*

THE U.S. CONSTITUTION is based on the concept of government under law. Under this system, the military cannot legitimately imprison civilians without review by civil courts. Even during war, the Constitution protects citizens against imprisonment without charges or trial. Yet such imprisonment was forced on 110,000 Japanese Americans on the West Coast during World War II. With the sanction of the president and Congress, the military removed these men, women, and children—most of whom were American citizens—from their homes and forced them to live in internment camps under armed guard. The U.S. Supreme Court, in a 1944 decision, *Korematsu v.*

United States, allowed the removal and imprisonment of these Americans because of "military necessity."

One of the three dissenters in the decision, Justice Frank Murphy, called the decision a "legalization of racism." He charged that the military action behind the suit was "one of the most sweeping and complete deprivations of constitutional rights in the history of this nation in the absence of martial law."

Critics of the opinion, then and now, have characterized the ruling as a low point in Supreme Court history. They note that the justices voting in the majority failed to demand convincing proof to support the government's claim of national security in revoking citizens' civil rights. As it turned out, there was no proof. The military judgment to intern American citizens of Japanese heritage was based solely on racial prejudice, according to the report of the Commission on Wartime Relocation and Internment of Civilians. Congress established the commission in 1980 to investigate the Japanese internment during World War II. Its in-depth report prompted President George H. W. Bush to issue an official apology to Japanese Americans in 1988 and pushed Congress to approve payments to victims of the relocation order.

Government documents uncovered in the 1980s by a lawyer/researcher proved that Japanese Americans never threatened national security. According to these papers, the government lawyers who presented the case to the U.S. Supreme Court knowingly covered up reports that contradicted the claims of military necessity. As a result of this discovery, a federal court cleared the name of Fred Toyosaburo Korematsu, whose original appeal brought the case before the U.S. Supreme Court in 1944.

Although the Supreme Court has never overturned the *Korematsu* ruling, the decision "lies overruled in the court of history," according to the 1980 Congressional Commission. Because of its link to wholesale racial stereotyping, most historians and legal experts look on the *Korematsu* ruling with disdain. In a majority opinion in a 1995 case involving preferential treatment for minority-owned businesses, Justice Sandra Day O'Connor noted the need for "the most searching judicial inquiry" to avoid "another such error" as the *Korematsu* ruling.

The nation, however, continues to face the troubling issues raised in the case, which pitted the guarantees of the Bill of Rights against the forces of racism, military might, national security claims, and public hysteria. In his sharp dissent to the *Korematsu* decision, Supreme Court Justice Robert Jackson warned that the Court's approval of the order to remove Japanese Americans from their homes, far more than the order itself, presented a continuing danger to our democratic society. He wrote:

> [O]nce a judicial opinion rationalizes such an order to show that it conforms to the Constitution, or rather rationalizes the Constitution to show that the Constitution sanctions such an order, the Court for all time has validated the principle of racial discrimination in criminal procedure and of transplanting American citizens. The principle then lies about like a loaded weapon ready for the hand of any authority that can bring forward a plausible claim of an urgent need.

Indeed, the *Korematsu* ruling has received a measure of support from Chief Justice William Rehnquist. Because the nation was at war, the chief justice argues in a recent book, the government had a legitimate right to act in the nation's defense against resident aliens. "In war, the law is silent," Rehnquist writes. "Without question, the government's authority to engage in conduct that infringes civil liberty is greatest in time of declared war." He does not defend discrimination against *citizens* of a particular ethnic background, however.

Historically, the Court has allowed the government and military leaders a freer hand during wartime. Civil libertarians have expressed the fear that the *Korematsu* ruling might be used to justify the George W. Bush administration's internment of citizens and aliens in its war against terrorism.

After Islamic terrorists attacked New York and the Pentagon in 2001, the Bush administration issued orders that terrorist suspects be interned without the usual evidence required by U.S. courts. Advocates for the jailed suspects sued, and in the spring of 2004 the U.S. Supreme Court reviewed the cases.

Once again, Fred Korematsu took a stand to protect the rights promised in the Constitution. In a brief filed in support of the detainees, Korematsu issued a plea for justice. His presence sent a powerful reminder of another dark time in the nation's history and emphasized the importance of standing up for individual rights, in peace and in war. Korematsu's epic journey continues to offer its warning lesson: A democracy, even one under attack, must preserve the rights and liberties assured citizens or risk losing the very freedoms for which soldiers sacrifice their lives. When courts give up the right to review military control of civilians, they upset the intricate balance of power fashioned by the country's founders to protect the American way of life.

one
"A Date Which Will Live in Infamy"

JUST BEFORE 8 a.m. on December 7, 1941, Japanese planes flew into Pearl Harbor, Hawaii, without warning and spewed armor-piercing bombs on the U.S. fleet based there. The surprise attack left twelve American ships sinking or beached; another nine were severely damaged. More than 2,400 Americans died in the bombing. More than 1,100 military personnel and civilians suffered injuries in the assault. It was "a date which will live in infamy," President Franklin D. Roosevelt told a shocked American public and Congress the following day. As of that moment, the president declared, the nation was at war with Japan.

For Americans across the nation, the terrible attack destroyed more than battleships or even human lives—it damaged citizens' sense of security. America was no longer a safe haven. Ripples of fear spread through cities and towns, especially those closest to Pearl Harbor. People believed that such an attack could happen again. Suspicion focused on Japanese Americans living on the West Coast. Many regarded them as the enemy because of their heritage. Even Japanese Americans who had been born in the United States, had never set foot in Japan, and could not speak Japanese became targets of distrust and scorn.

FRED KOREMATSU, CENTER, STANDS WITH HIS FAMILY IN THE KOREMATSUS' GREENHOUSE.

The day Japan bombed Pearl Harbor, Fred Korematsu and his Italian-American girlfriend had driven to Skyline Boulevard above San Francisco and were enjoying the view of the city and listening to the car radio. "We had spread out the Sunday magazine, the *Tribune*, and I just relaxed and had the music on. . . . [It was] Sunday, a nice sunny day," he reminisced. Then the radio fell silent. At first, the twenty-two-year-old American-born Korematsu thought he might be dreaming the news reporter's urgent announcement of a Japanese invasion at Pearl Harbor.

However, as the announcer gave vivid details of the attack—bombs falling, people dead and injured—Korematsu realized the report was true.

At home, his parents listened to the reports with growing dread. They feared the family would become a target because of their Japanese ancestry. That fear, they soon learned, would be well justified. When young Korematsu, a welder, reported for work at the local shipyard the Monday after Pearl Harbor, his union informed him he no longer had a job. Within days, police knocked on the door and confiscated the Korematsus' cameras and flashlights to prevent them from signaling the enemy. Those actions marked the beginning of years of unjust treatment and indignities inflicted on the family and other West Coast Japanese Americans.

A HISTOrY OF RaCISM

Discrimination against Asians was not new. Beginning in the mid–1800s, Chinese laborers came to the United States to build railroads, operate fishing vessels, and work in factories, farms, and mines. By 1870, Chinese immigrants made up one-fifth of California's work force. After a depression hit the nation in 1876, reaction against the Chinese workers led Congress to pass the Chinese Exclusion Act. The 1882 law banned all Chinese workers from immigrating to the United States. Under the law, no person of Chinese descent could become a U.S. citizen. Severe limits on Chinese immigration remained in effect for the next sixty years.

With the exclusion of Chinese workers, Japanese immigrants began entering the United States seeking work in the late 1800s. Like the Chinese before them, Japanese workers filled low-paying jobs in California and other western states. They, too, became targets of dis-

IT'S ALL YOUR FAULT: A SCAPEGOAT FOR ALL SEASONS

During every period of crisis, some people direct their fear and hatred toward minority groups. This is especially true during war, when fearful citizens may extend their hatred of the enemy to those Americans whose ancestors migrated from the enemy land. Here are examples of such scapegoating through the years:

ITALIAN AMERICANS, 1911

The South Italians are slow in becoming Americanized and many in the coal regions who have been in this country from fifteen to twenty years are scarcely able to speak English. They live in colonies, have very little association with natives, and show little interest outside of their own immediate neighborhood. They are suspicious of Americans, do not trust their money to the banks, and trade at American shops as little as possible. They are making little progress toward Americanization.

Study on Italian Americans by the U.S. Congress

GERMAN AMERICANS, IRISH AMERICANS, OTHER IMMIGRANTS, 1915

Those hyphenated Americans who terrorize American politicians by threats of the foreign vote are engaged in treason to the American Republic.

Former U.S. President Theodore Roosevelt
in a speech before the Knights of Columbus

GERMAN AMERICANS, WORLD WAR I

Do not become a tool of the [enemy] by passing on the malicious, disheartening rumors which he so eagerly sows. Remember he asks no better service than to have you spread his lies of disasters to our soldiers. And do not wait until you catch someone putting a bomb under a factory. Report the man who spreads pessimistic stories, divulges—or seeks—confidential military information, cries for peace or belittles our efforts to win the war.

U.S. Justice Department pamphlet aimed at German Americans and those critical of the war effort

German Americans, Irish Americans, Other Immigrants, 1919

Any man who carries a hyphen about with him carries a dagger that he is ready to plunge into the vitals of this Republic whenever he gets ready.

U.S. President Woodrow Wilson in a speech supporting the League of Nations at Pueblo, Colorado, September 25, 1919

Japanese Americans, 1942

We will have to bear another catastrophe before we awake to the fact that they will stop at nothing, that as a nation they have no Christian morality, no honor, sympathy, no human feeling for other humans.

R. L. Fairbank in a letter to the San Diego City Council regarding the threat posed by Japanese Americans

Muslims, 2001

I don't believe [Islam] is a wonderful, peaceful religion. When you read the Koran and you read the verses from the Koran, it instructs the killing of the infidel, for those that are non-Muslim . . . It wasn't Methodists flying into those buildings, it wasn't Lutherans. It was an attack on this country by people of the Islamic faith.

Franklin Graham, evangelist, after September 11, 2001, attacks on New York's World Trade Center and the Pentagon

MUSLIMS, 2002

"There is no such thing as peaceful Islam. Islamics cannot fit into an America in which the first loyalty is to the American Constitution. They should be encouraged to leave. They are a fifth column in this country."

William Lind of the Free Congress Foundation

crimination. In several areas, all "pupils of the Mongolian [Asian] race" had to attend segregated schools. In 1907, under pressure from American diplomats, Japan agreed not to issue any more passports to Japanese workers wishing to immigrate to America. Wives and children, however, could join men already in the United States. In return, the United States agreed not to pass a law specifically excluding Japanese workers.

Once in the United States, Japanese immigrants built homes, established churches, and set up social organizations. About half of the Japanese immigrants on U.S. territory lived in Hawaii. A majority of the rest settled in California. Many bought land rejected by other residents and through hard work grew crops on it. By 1920, Japanese farmers oversaw more than 450,000 acres in California and earned more than 10 percent of the revenue from that state's harvests. Their success in farming aroused jealousy among their neighbors. They became targets of groups like the American Federation of Labor and local agitators who pushed for anti-Japanese legislation.

In 1924, Congress passed the Immigration Act, banning most immigrants from Japan. The law also prohibited U.S. immigrants born in Japan—known as Issei—from becoming American citizens. Local leaders passed laws forbidding Japanese aliens (noncitizens) from owning land. To circumvent the law, many families transferred their land to their children. While the law barred Issei from citizenship, the Fourteenth Amendment guaranteed that their children born in the United States would automatically be American citizens. This second generation of Japanese Americans became known as Nisei. Another group of Japanese Americans—the Kibei—were American-born citizens whose parents sent them to schools in Japan during their

UNITED STATES DEPARTMENT OF JUSTICE

★

NOTICE
TO ALIENS OF ENEMY
NATIONALITIES

★ The United States Government requires all aliens
of German, Italian, or Japanese nationality to apply
at post offices nearest to their place of residence for a
Certificate of Identification. Applications must be filed
between the period February 9 through February 28, 1942.
Go to your postmaster today for printed directions.

EARL G. HARRISON,
Special Assistant to the Attorney General.

FRANCIS BIDDLE,
Attorney General.

AVVISO

Il Governo degli Stati Uniti ordina a tutti gli
stranieri di nazionalità Tedesca, Italiana e Giap-
ponese di fare richiesta all' Ufficio Postale più
prossimo al loro luogo di residenza per ottenere
un Certificato d'Identità. Le richieste devono
essere fatte entro il periodo che decorre tra il 9
Febbraio e il 28 Febbraio, 1942.
*Andate oggi dal vostro Capo d'Ufficio Postale
(Postmaster) per ricevere le istruzioni scritte.*

BEKANNTMACHUNG

Die Regierung der Vereinigten Staaten von
Amerika fordert alle Auslaender deutscher, ita-
lienischer und japanischer Staatsangehoerigkeit
auf, sich auf das ihrem Wohnorte naheliegende
Postamt zu begeben, um einen Personalausweis
zu beantragen. Das Gesuch muss zwischen dem
9. und 28. Februar 1942 eingereicht werden.
*Gehen Sie noch heute zu Ihrem Postmeister
und verschaffen Sie sich die gedruckten Vor-
schriften.*

敵國外人注意

日獨伊諸國ノ國籍ヲ有スル在雷外人ハ
二月九日ヨリ二十八日マデノ間ニ其居所ニ一番
近イ郵便局デ自分證明書ヲ申込ム可シ。
合モ早速郵便局ヘ行キテ説明書ヲ賴ミ樣ニ願ヒマス。

Post This Side In All States EXCEPT
Arizona, California, Idaho, Montana, Nevada, Oregon, Utah, Washington

---

This Department of Justice notice, posted in February 1942, informs
all noncitizens from Germany, Italy, or Japan to register at their
local post office. The poster was the first step in compiling a list
of all resident aliens from the three countries at war with the
United States.

childhood. Because of their close association with Japan, the Kibei would be subjected to even more indignities than other Japanese Americans.

Many of the new generation of Japanese Americans spoke English, attended Christian churches, and cheered sports teams alongside their non-Asian friends.

TWO
"A VIPER IS NONETHELESS A VIPER"

WITH THE BOMBING of Pearl Harbor, once-friendly neighbors became hostile to Japanese Americans. It made no difference if a Japanese-American citizen had been raised in the United States, had never set foot in Japan, and could not speak Japanese. All those of Asian ancestry became suspect. In the eyes of many fearful West Coast residents, Japanese Americans became the "fifth column" of Japan's army. The term refers to secret supporters of the enemy who act as spies within the nation where they live. No evidence of such activity among Japanese Americans in Hawaii or on the West Coast has ever surfaced. Nevertheless, anti-Asian forces used the accusations to fan the flames of racial hatred.

Officials took quick action against those they considered "enemy" aliens. The Justice Department investigated German, Japanese, and Italian immigrants they suspected of treachery. Many belonged to organizations that the FBI considered suspicious. Police arrested community leaders, teachers in Japanese schools, and members of civic organizations because of their connection to Japanese heritage. Families rushed to destroy any evidence of their links to Japan. Suyako Kitashima recalled burning the family's treasures in the backyard. "We had to have a bonfire . . . and burn everything that resembled Japan, even if

Deputy sheriffs frisk two Japanese-American men at the police station in Los Angeles after widespread raids in California in March 1942 targeted members of the Asian community. Police and military officers took into custody between 150 and 200 Japanese Americans suspected of helping enemy forces. The government failed to produce solid evidence of treason against the United States by even one Japanese American during World War II.

it was a picture of your uncle in Japan in Japanese clothes. My mother burned everything, even calendars. Anything written in Japanese made you a suspect."

Police barred suspects from sensitive areas along both coasts. Some were arrested and sent to internment camps. Once there, the detainees sat through hearings held to determine their loyalty. They had no lawyers, but they could present evidence and witnesses to support their innocence.

By February 16, 1942, officials had detained 2,192 Japanese, 1,393 Germans, and 264 Italians. The government's treatment of Japanese Americans differed radically from that accorded people of German and Italian ancestry. Officials arrested a limited number of enemy aliens of other nationalities. Many of the arrests were based on actions and behavior by individuals or small associations. On the other hand, the entire population of West Coast Japanese Americans fell under suspicion. Shortly after Pearl Harbor, military and civilian forces began to push for the removal of all ethnic Japanese including those who were American citizens—from the West Coast.

There were several reasons for this difference in treatment. Logistically, it would have been extremely difficult to relocate the one million German and Italian immigrants living in the United States. Fewer than 120,000 Japanese Americans lived in communities along the West Coast. Racial discrimination also played a role. Germans and Italians were seen as "thoroughly Americanized" and "as a group are loyal to the American war effort," according to the report of the Tolan Committee, charged by Congress to investigate the situation. Japanese Americans looked different, were members of a different race from the majority of Americans, and many practiced a non-Christian religion. California Attorney General Earl Warren (later chief justice of the U.S. Supreme Court) cited these differences during testimony before the Tolan Committee. He argued that it was impossible for officials to determine whether Japanese Americans were loyal to the United States:

> We believe that when we are dealing with the Caucasian race we have methods that will test the loyalty of them, and we believe that we can, in dealing with the Germans and Italians, arrive at some fairly sound conclusions because of our knowledge of the way they live in the community and have lived for many years. But when we deal

with the Japanese we are in an entirely different field and we can not form any opinion that we believe to be sound.

Unlike Germans and Italians, immigrants from Japan were barred by law from becoming American citizens. They had little political power; most of those born in the United States (and who were therefore citizens) were not old enough to vote.

In addition, some West Coast businessmen resented the success of Japanese-American farmers and stood to benefit from their removal. During the Tolan Committee hearings, conducted on the West Coast in February and March of 1942, more than one person testified that white business interests stood behind the campaign to evacuate Japanese Americans from the area. "The great cry of 'Kick the Japanese out of the Yakima Valley' is not due to fear of sabotage, it is due to economic reasons," a Washington university student told the committee. A California attorney and a representative of the Japanese American Citizens League expressed similar views to the committee.

After attacking Pearl Harbor, Japan's army took control of the war in the Pacific. The Malay Peninsula, Hong Kong, Thailand, Guam, and finally the Philippines fell, as Japan posted victory after victory. Japan's war triumphs served to intensify feelings against Japanese Americans.

The local press quickly stirred up fear and hatred among West Coast residents. Most newspapers unabashedly reflected the public's hostile views toward Japanese Americans. They spread rumors under banner headlines. Among the stories were unsubstantiated reports of a Japanese spy ring in Los Angeles, a raid on U.S. ships by Japanese submarines off the California

U.S. INTERNMENT OF GERMANS, ITALIANS, AND OTHER FOREIGN NATIONALS

Japanese Americans were not the only group to be interned by the U.S. government. Thousands of German, Italian, and other immigrants were sent to prison camps in the United States during World War I and World War II.

Shortly after the United States declared war on Germany during World War I, President Woodrow Wilson issued twelve regulations that applied to "enemy aliens." These so-called aliens were U.S. residents who had been born in Germany and had not yet become American citizens (also known as foreign nationals).

The regulations severely restricted the aliens' movements and authorized the Justice Department to arrest German aliens suspected of aiding the enemy. German Americans could be arrested on grounds of being a "danger" to "the public peace or safety" or merely because an officer suspected they were "about to violate" any regulation issued by the president.

By the end of October 1917, about nine hundred German Americans had been arrested and were being held in internment camps in Georgia and Utah.

In November 1917 Wilson issued eight more regulations that established exclusion zones from which enemy aliens were banned. Under the proclamation, aliens had to register with the government and could be prevented from moving or changing jobs. The following month, after Congress declared war on Austria-Hungary, natives of that region were also labeled enemy aliens to whom the restrictions applied.

Government officials arrested thousands in the

spring of 1918. Many had committed no crime other than being in an exclusion zone or belonging to a group that federal agents believed was suspicious. Members of socialist groups, Jehovah's Witnesses, conscientious objectors, and "undesirables" (including those who spoke out publicly against the administration) were also arrested and imprisoned in the camps.

Congress backed Wilson's measures with the passage of the Espionage Act of 1917 and the Sedition Act a year later. Both took aim against enemies within the United States. Under the Espionage Act, protesters could be arrested for "any disloyal, profane, scurrilous, or abusive language about the form of government . . . the Constitution . . . or the flag of the United States, or the uniform of the Army and Navy."

Arrests continued even after the armistice was signed on November 1918. By February 1919, when the last arrests were made, more than six thousand people lived at the camps under armed guard. The government released about one-third of the prisoners in the spring of 1919. Another third chose to be deported to their native land, even though some had not lived there since early childhood. The U.S. government finally closed the camps in May 1920 because of financial pressures.

During World War II, President Franklin D. Roosevelt's proclamations affected Germans and Italians living in the United States as well as those of Japanese descent. Germans and Italians who lived in the United States but were not American citizens had to register with the federal government. After the attack on Pearl Harbor, thousands were arrested and questioned. They were excluded from sensitive military zones, required to follow curfews, and barred from traveling. The exclusion orders also applied to U.S. citizens of German descent considered to be "potentially dangerous" by the government. The government did not subject American citizens of German and Italian descent to mass detention, however. Some of these citizens were arrested and interned, but unlike their Japanese-American counterparts, they were sent to camps only after individual warrants had been issued in their names.

By war's end, at least 11,000 German residents had been imprisoned in internment camps. In 1942, the United States exchanged about two thousand of the German internees and their families for American prisoners of war being held in Germany.

Government officials also questioned about 2,700 Italian residents and sent three hundred of them to Fort Missoula, Montana, where they were imprisoned with about 1,200 Italian sailors and visitors from Italy.

coast, and suspicious flares and blinkers that worried navy officers. Readers were told how to protect themselves in case of poison gas attacks. One article reported that California Governor Culbert Olson feared the Japanese might soon attack the state.

In an editorial published in the *Santa Cruz Sentinel-News* eleven days after the bombing, writer Ernest Hauser suggested that Japanese-American citizens who as children had studied at schools in Japan could well be spies for the enemy.

> They [the Kibei] are imbued with the spirit of Nippon, with its strong elements of loyalty to the Emperor and to the Rising Sun. What would be easier for Japan's military and naval authorities than to send some of them over here with appropriate instructions?

Another editorial, published in the *Los Angeles Times*, suggested that Japanese-American citizens were really Japanese. "A viper is nonetheless a viper wherever the egg is hatched," the author W. H. Anderson wrote. Many newspapers referred to Japanese Americans as "Japs," "Nippons," or by other pejorative terms.

Political leaders began calling for an evacuation from the West Coast of all those of Japanese ancestry. Some suggested that all Japanese Americans be imprisoned. Santa Cruz Mayor Edwin L. Rich told a news reporter that the citizens of his city "would feel a lot safer with all Japanese out of the community." In the same edition of the paper, U.S. Congressman John Elliott Rankin, D-Mississippi, is quoted as saying, "Once a Jap, always a Jap." He went on to urge the government to put "every Japanese . . . in a concentration camp." Fellow Congressman John Martin

Costello, D-California, also supported an evacuation that would include American citizens of Japanese descent. "The only solution," he said, "is to remove from the area completely those persons who are likely to commit sabotage."

By February, West Coast newspapers featured daily lists of leaders who supported an evacuation of Japanese Americans. Among them were members of Congress, the Los Angeles County Defense Council, Ventura County officials, mayors and other city officials, Attorney General Warren, and Governor Olson. The League of California Cities called for its members to pass resolutions supporting the removal of Japanese Americans from the West Coast. A number of West Coast cities did just that.

Esteemed reporter Walter Lippman, in a column headlined "The Fifth Column on the Coast," sounded an alarm against Japanese-American spies. Repeating warnings that the West Coast might "at any moment" come under attack, he joined the chorus of those calling for evacuation of Japanese Americans. "Nobody's constitutional rights include the right to reside and do business on a battlefield," he wrote. "And nobody ought to be on a battlefield who has no good reason for being there." Lippman acknowledged that there had been "no important sabotage on the Pacific Coast." But he used that fact to bolster his case against Japanese Americans. Under his twisted logic, the lack of any evidence against this group merely proved that the Japanese-American spies were well organized and getting ready for treachery. According to Lippman, they planned to attack when it would have "maximum effect." Military experts would also use this rationale to justify their suspicions of Japanese Americans.

In the turmoil after the Pearl Harbor attack, Japanese schools on the West Coast closed, banks and businesses were seized, and Japanese immigrants were ordered to turn over their radios and cameras. On

January 14, 1942, President Roosevelt ordered the regis-
tration of all Japanese who were not citizens (including
all of the Issei, since they were not allowed citizenship).
Los Angeles city and county officials fired all employees
of Japanese ancestry.

searches and seizures

Even before the attack on Pearl Harbor, the War
Department (later the Department of Defense) had begun
to coordinate the nation's defense forces. In March 1941
the War Department divided the country into four sections,
or defense commands, each under the control of an army
officer. The commands (Northeast, Central, Southern, and
Western) controlled both air and ground forces and
assumed responsibility for defending their areas.

Lieutenant General John L. DeWitt oversaw security
for the West Coast as the officer in charge of the Western
Defense Command. The area included the entire Pacific
coast region, Arizona, and several other western states.
After Pearl Harbor, he pushed for wholesale searches of
Japanese-American homes and businesses. The Justice
Department, which traditionally guarded citizens' rights
against unwarranted searches and seizures, resisted.
Since the West Coast was not a war zone, the Justice
Department rather than the War Department controlled
the civilian population there.

Attorney General Francis Biddle, head of Justice,
eventually approved a roundup of resident aliens who fell
into certain suspicious categories. Arrests of citizens,
however, could only be made if officials had probable
cause that they had committed a crime. As fears escalated,
Biddle gave in to DeWitt's demand that enemy aliens be
banned from certain military areas on the West Coast. In
addition, Biddle set up curfews in other areas in
California, which went into effect February 4.

Biddle later regretted his role in the ban and eventual evacuation of Japanese Americans. In his 1962 memoir, Biddle wrote, "I thought at the time that the [evacuation] program was ill-advised, unnecessary, and unnecessarily cruel." He said he bent to political pressure because of his high regard for Secretary of War Henry Stimson, who also went along with the evacuation. "If . . . I had urged the Secretary to resist the pressure of his subordinates, the result might have been different. But I was new to the Cabinet, and disinclined to insist on my view to an elder statesman whose wisdom and integrity I greatly respected."

Immediately after the Japanese raid on Pearl Harbor, President Roosevelt appointed a commission headed by Supreme Court Justice Owen Roberts to investigate the attack. The commission issued its report at the end of January. According to the report, Japanese spies on the island of Oahu had sent U.S. military information to Japan before the attack. Some of these spies, the commission reported, were affiliated with the Japanese consulate; others had "no open relations with the Japanese foreign service." This latter group, presumably, consisted of Japanese Americans living in Hawaii. The report presented no evidence to back the allegation and went no further in investigating ethnic Japanese living on the island.

President Roosevelt placed Hawaii, then a U.S. territory, under martial law after the attack on Pearl Harbor. The military imposed curfews and travel restrictions on all Hawaiian residents.* These actions did not satisfy some politicians, who proposed that all ethnic Japanese in Hawaii be jailed. General Delos Emmons, the military

---

* The federal judge overseeing Hawaii later criticized the military's conduct in the islands. Authorities had the power to declare martial law, the judge noted, but the army "set up that which was lawful only in conquered enemy territory namely, military government which is not bound by the Constitution. And they . . . threw the Constitution into the discard and set up a military dictatorship."

commander in charge of Hawaii, argued against such a move. He noted that there was no evidence that Japanese Americans on the islands had been involved in sabotage. At the time, Japanese Americans made up about one-third of the islands' population. To jail them would have taken manpower and money from vital military operations, Emmons contended. And since Japanese Americans supplied most of the islands' labor, taking them from their jobs would have severely hampered the military's operations. Officials in Washington, D.C., accepted Emmons's assessment and took no further action against Hawaii's Japanese population.

On the West Coast, however, a different scenario was unfolding. DeWitt remained convinced that Japanese Americans represented a threat to national security, even though he had no evidence of treachery. On February 14, 1942, he sent a memo to Secretary of War Henry Stimson urging that all "Japanese and other subversive persons" be removed from the West Coast. He gave several reasons for his recommendation. The first focused on the general's stereotypical racial views. According to him, Japanese people could not assimilate into American culture. They belonged to "an enemy race," whose "racial strains [were] undiluted." Potentially, all 110,000 or so people of Japanese ancestry living on the West Coast (many of whom were children) could turn against the United States. The Japanese Americans' alien nature, DeWitt claimed, made it impossible to determine who among them were enemies. He cited vague "indications" but no proof that the ethnic Japanese were organized and "ready for concerted action at a favorable opportunity." Like columnist Lippman, he used the illogical argument that the lack of acts of sabotage by Japanese Americans confirmed they planned such action.

DeWitt added other justifications in his *Final Report* on the evacuation, released in 1944. He cited examples of signals transmitted from shore to Japanese submarines and weapons found during searches of Japanese homes. The Federal Communications Commission (FCC) had already investigated the report of signals and had discounted it. While the Federal Bureau of Investigation (FBI) had found some weapons, most were ordinary shotguns that farmers would normally own.

DeWitt argued that evacuation would protect Japanese Americans from mob violence. According to Congressional records of the time, however, only thirty-six cases of violence against West Coast Japanese Americans were reported in the three-month period following the Pearl Harbor attack. The general also listed features of Japanese culture that he believed made the population suspect: schools that taught the Japanese language, ethnic organizations, the Shinto religion, and the practice of sending children to study in Japan. He offered no proof that any of these factors led to enemy activity.

In fact, most Japanese Americans living on the West Coast were either Buddhists or Christians. Only a small number followed the state Shinto religion that gained power in Japan in the 1930s. More a political platform than a religion, state Shinto treated the Japanese emperor as a god and preached unquestioning loyalty to Japan. That made its followers suspect, in the military's view.

opponents of evacuation

A few top officials in the Roosevelt administration, including Justice Department lawyers and First Lady Eleanor Roosevelt, opposed an evacuation and other drastic measures being considered. Shortly after the attack on Pearl Harbor, Eleanor Roosevelt had flown to the West Coast to help boost the morale of civilian defense workers. While there, she had made a point of posing with

Japanese Americans and spoke out against unfairly targeting loyal Americans who happened to belong to minority groups. She addressed the issue in her weekly newspaper column as well. Her words drew a virulent response from the *Los Angeles Times*. The editorial writer chastised her for "bemoaning the plight of the treacherous snakes we call Japanese." In response, Eleanor Roosevelt wrote another column defending her position and emphasizing the importance of the Bill of Rights. "I think almost the biggest obligation we have today," she wrote, "is to prove that in a time of stress we can still live up to our beliefs and maintain the civil liberties we have established as the rights of human beings everywhere."

Lawyers in the Justice Department also disagreed with the proposed handling of the West Coast situation. They

First Lady Eleanor Roosevelt chats with Japanese-American teens in Tacoma, Washington, on December 14, 1941, one week after Japan's attack on Pearl Harbor. The young people were members of the Japanese-American Citizens Defense Committee.

argued that a Japanese-American evacuation violated the rights guaranteed in the U.S. Constitution. But their opinions carried little weight against the aggressive arguments presented by the president's military advisers. U.S. Attorney General Biddle initially opposed the decision but, like the rest of the Cabinet, he ultimately went along with it.

FBI director J. Edgar Hoover did not believe the evacuation of Japanese Americans was necessary or justified. His agents had found no evidence of sabotage among the West Coast Japanese-American population. Nor did they find any proof that Japanese Americans in Hawaii had helped the Japanese in the Pearl Harbor attack. In fact, immediately after the attack, Japanese Americans had led rescue efforts in Hawaii. Hoover believed that agents could identify enemy aliens without having to intern thousands of innocent people.

Neither did the majority of the American public embrace the harsh measures promoted by the military and anti-Japanese forces. A secret report on a poll conducted for the government in early 1942 showed that anti-Japanese-American sentiment was not as prevalent as articles in the newspapers might indicate. With the exception of southern California residents, fewer than 50 percent of those interviewed supported internment of Japanese immigrants (noncitizens). Only 14 percent believed American citizens of Japanese descent should be interned.

roosevelt signs the order

In the end, however, President Roosevelt responded to the loud urgings of frightened California residents, anti-Japanese reports in West Coast newspapers, pressure from politicians, and the demands of the military. On

February 19, 1942, he issued Executive Order Number 9066. The order did not specifically target Japanese Americans, but it allowed the military to set up military zones "from which any or all persons may be excluded." The order also empowered military leaders to determine who could "enter, remain in, or leave" these areas. This set the stage for the mass evacuation of Japanese Americans that would follow.

The president's decision to issue the executive order contradicted everything Eleanor Roosevelt had been saying about tolerance and human rights. Historian Doris Kearns Goodwin wrote that the First Lady was greatly dismayed by the president's action. When she tried to discuss her objections with her husband, however, he ordered her not to mention the subject again.

On February 20, the day after the president issued the executive order, Secretary of War Stimson put General John L. DeWitt in charge of carrying it out. DeWitt lost no time in taking control. On March 2, the general issued Proclamation No. 1. The order designated the western half of California, Oregon, and Washington, and the southern third of Arizona as Military Area No. 1, from which Japanese Americans would be excluded. DeWitt labeled the remaining area of the four states as Military Area No. 2. DeWitt told the press that the army would first require ethnic Japanese, alien and citizen alike, to leave Area No. 1. Only after that had been accomplished would the army turn its efforts to removal of German and Italian aliens (but not citizens). Area No. 2 would presumably remain open to all.

Although DeWitt made it clear that Japanese Americans would be excluded from Area No. 1, he did not detail how that would be accomplished. Officials originally hoped Japanese Americans would leave

EXECUTIVE ORDER NO. 9066

FEBRUARY 19, 1942
AUTHORIZING THE SECRETARY OF WAR TO PRESCRIBE MILITARY AREAS

Whereas, the successful prosecution of the war requires every possible protection against espionage and against sabotage to national defense material, national defense premises and national defense utilities as defined in Section 4, Act of April 20, 1918, 40 Stat. 533 as amended by the Act of November 30, 1940, 54 Stat. 1220. and the Act of August 21, 1941. 55 Stat. 655 (U.S.C., Title 50, Sec. 104):

Now, therefore, by virtue of the authority vested in me as President of the United States, and Commander in Chief of the Army and Navy, I hereby authorize and direct the Secretary of War, and the Military Commanders whom he may from time to time designate, whenever he or any designated Commander deem such action necessary or desirable to prescribe military areas in such places and of such extent as he or the appropriate Military Commander may determine, from which any or all persons may be excluded, and with respect to which, the right of any person to enter, remain in, or leave shall be subject to whatever restriction the Secretary of War or the appropriate Military Commander may impose in his discretion. The Secretary of War is hereby authorized to provide for residents of any such area who are excluded therefrom. such transportation, food, shelter, and other accommodations as may be necessary, in the judgment of the Secretary of War or the said Military Commander and until other arrangements are made, to accomplish the purpose of this order. The designation of military areas in any region or locality shall supersede designation of prohibited and restricted areas by the Attorney General under the Proclamation of December 7 and 8, 1941, and shall supersede the responsibility and authority of the Attorney General under the said Proclamation in respect of such prohibited and restricted areas.

I hereby further authorize and direct the Secretary of War and the said Military Commanders to take such other steps as he or the appropriate Military Commander may deem advisable to enforce compliance with the restrictions applicable to each Military area herein above authorized to be designated. including the use of Federal troops and other Federal Agencies, with authority to accept assistance of state and local agencies.

I hereby further authorize and direct all Executive Department, independent establishments and other Federal Agencies, to assist the Secretary of War or the said Military Commanders in carrying out this Executive Order, including the furnishing of medical aid, hospitalization, food, clothing, transportation, use of land, shelter, and other supplies, equipment, utilities, facilities and service.

This order shall not be construed as modifying or limiting in any way the authority granted under

Executive Order 8972, dated December 12, 1941, nor shall it be construed as limiting or modifying the duty and responsibility of the Federal Bureau of Investigation, with response to the investigation of alleged acts of sabotage or duty and responsibility of the Attorney General and the Department of Justice under the Proclamation of December 7 and 8, 1941, prescribing regulations for the conduct and control of alien enemies, except as such duty and responsibility is superseded by the designation of military areas thereunder.

Franklin D. Roosevelt
The White House, February 19, 1942

voluntarily. Some had already moved out of the military zones designated by Biddle in January. It soon became apparent, however, that a voluntary system would not work. Most of the Japanese Americans living on the West Coast had nowhere else to go. Governors of several states had made it clear they did not want them in their territory. Nevada Governor Edward Peter Carville wrote that Japanese Americans moving to his state would have to be under strict supervision or in concentration camps. Colorado's governor pledged that the state would take its share of displaced aliens, but only as a way to help the nation's war effort, not as a humanitarian act.

Japanese Americans who did move had to leave behind their businesses, homes, and possessions. What little they managed to sell brought only bargain-basement prices. The government had closed down the Japanese banks where many Japanese Americans did business shortly after the Pearl Harbor attack. That made it even more difficult to settle their financial affairs before leaving the area.

Several local and regional authorities began pushing for harsher measures, including forced removal and internment of Japanese Americans. The County Supervisors Association of California advised its members to pass a resolution to remove the West Coast Japanese Americans and confine them in inland areas. The Board of Supervisors of San Diego County approved a similar measure. California's American Legion also supported internment, and the Grange went on record in support of a full-scale removal of the Japanese-American population from the entire West Coast.

Tolan Committee Hearings

Congress took action by assigning the Select Committee Investigating National Defense Migration, headed by U.S.

Representative John H. Tolan, D-California, to study the need for an evacuation. Immediately after Roosevelt issued Executive Order 9066, the committee opened hearings on the West Coast. From late February through early March, the panel—known as the Tolan Committee—heard testimony from a wide range of people.

California Attorney General Earl Warren headlined the list of those appearing before the committee. His testimony echoed many of General DeWitt's statements. Warren suggested sinister motives behind the fact that Japanese farms circled many of the strategic military posts in the area. But others noted that most of the farms had been in place since 1910. The attorney general also repeated the contention that since no sabotage had occurred yet, Japanese Americans must be preparing to act soon.

Shortly after the Pearl Harbor attack, Secretary of the Navy Frank Knox had announced that Japanese living in Hawaii had been a major help to the enemy. The members of the Tolan Committee accepted this statement as fact. At one hearing, John Tolan stated that Japan "had probably the greatest, the most perfect system of espionage and sabotage ever in the history of war, native-born Japanese."

Certainly the evidence did not back up the claim. Honolulu's chief of police, FBI director Hoover, and civic leaders in Hawaii all testified that there had been no acts of sabotage at the hands of Japanese Americans. Even Secretary of War Stimson and Secretary of Navy Knox acknowledged they had no proof of any such acts.

Committee members also heard from a number of people opposed to the evacuation. College students spoke out in support of fellow classmates who were of Japanese ancestry. College professors, social workers, and religious leaders condemned removal of people based on race.

Rejecting the stance of many of his fellow mayors, Harry P. Cain, mayor of Tacoma, Washington, testified against an evacuation.

Officials of the Japanese American Citizens League (JACL) found themselves in an awkward position. As representatives of Japanese Americans, they had pledged their support to President Roosevelt immediately after the Pearl Harbor attack. Appearing before the committee, they reiterated their loyalty to the United States. If the nation's safety depended on the evacuation of Japanese Americans, then "we will have no hesitation in complying with [the plan]," JACL's national secretary, Mike Masaoka, told committee members. But loyal Japanese Americans should be treated like other citizens, he said. If political pressure, and not national security, inspired the plan, he added, then "we feel that we have every right to protest and to demand equitable judgment on our merits as American citizens."

In February 1942, Masaoka pledged the organization's support to the American government:

> We are preparing our people to move out. Why jeopardize this country or our people by trying to insist on staying, or even by pursuing our legal rights as citizens of this country to contest evacuation?

Throughout the war, the JACL urged Japanese Americans to cooperate with U.S. officials in an effort to prove their loyalty to the United States. That reasoning led the JACL to advise members not to participate in test cases protesting curfews, evacuation, and other actions directed at Japanese Americans. Inside the camps, JACL officials worked with administrators to quell dissent and encourage cooperation among the detainees. Critics would later condemn the JACL for working with the government and not taking a stronger stand against evacuation and imprisonment of Japanese Americans.

preparing for removal

By March the government had begun setting up detention (or "assembly") centers, where Japanese Americans moving from Area No. 1 could be housed temporarily. The first group had moved voluntarily, but DeWitt made it clear that other Japanese Americans living in the restricted zone would soon be forced to leave their homes. On March 11, DeWitt set up the Wartime Civil Control Administration (WCCA) to oversee the evacuation. On March 16, the WCCA extended the restricted military zones to sections of Idaho, Montana, Utah, and Nevada.

Executive Order 9066 had already empowered DeWitt to carry out an evacuation. But President Roosevelt signaled the government's willingness to force a mass evacuation when he issued Executive Order No. 9102 on March 18. The order set up a civilian board, the War Relocation Authority (WRA), and authorized it to work with other government agencies in removing "the persons or classes of persons" already referred to in the president's previous order. It also instructed the WRA to "provide for the relocation of such persons in appropriate places, provide for their needs in such manner as may be appropriate, and supervise their activities."

In addition, the order provided that WRA officials would help find work for those detained and assist them in disposing of their property. In issuing the order, Roosevelt said the removal would be done with "humane and constructive treatment" of the evacuees.

The order made no mention of forced confinement in prison camps.

civilian exclusion order
NO. 5
WESTERN DEFENSE COMMAND AND FOURTH ARMY
WARTIME CIVIL CONTROL ADMINISTRATION
Presidio of San Francisco, California
April 1, 1942

INSTRUCTIONS
TO ALL PERSONS OF
JAPANESE
ANCESTRY
LIVING IN THE FOLLOWING AREA:

All Japanese persons, both alien and non-alien, will be evacuated from the above designated area by 12 :00 o'clock noon, Tuesday, April 7, 1942.

No Japanese person will be permitted to enter or leave the above described area after 8:00 a. m., Thursday, April 2, 1942, without obtaining special permission from the Provost Marshal at the Civil Control Station located at:
1701 Van Ness Avenue
San Francisco, California

The Civil Control Station is equipped to assist the Japanese population affected by this evacuation in the following ways:

1. Give advice and instructions on the evacuation.

2. Provide services with respect to the management, leasing, sale, storage or other disposition of most kinds of property including: real estate, business and professional equipment, buildings, household goods, boats, automobiles, livestock, etc.

3. Provide temporary residence elsewhere for all Japanese in family groups.

4. Transport persons and a limited amount of clothing and equipment to their new residence, as specified below.

**THE FOLLOWING INSTRUCTIONS
MUST BE OBSERVED:**

1. A responsible member of each family, preferably the head of the family, or the person in whose name most of the property is held, and each individual living alone, will report to the Civil Control Station to receive further instructions. This must be done between 8:00 a. m. and 5:00 p. m., Thursday, April 2, 1942, or between 8:00 a. m. and 5 :00 p.m., Friday, April 3, 1942.

2. Evacuees must carry with them on departure for the Reception Center, the following property:

    a. Bedding and linens (no mattress) for each member of the family;

    b. Toilet articles for each member of the family;

    c. Extra clothing for each member of the family;

    d. Sufficient knives, forks, spoons, plates, bowls and cups for each member of the family;

    e. Essential personal effects for each member of the family.

All items carried will be securely packaged, tied and plainly marked with the name of the owner and numbered in accordance with instructions received at the Civil Control Station.

The size and number of packages is limited to that which can be carried by the individual or family group.

No contraband items as described in paragraph 6, Public Proclamation No. 3, Headquarters Western Defense Command and Fourth Army, dated March 24, 1942, will be carried.

3. The United States Government through its agencies will provide for the storage at the sole risk of the owner of the more substantial household items, such as iceboxes, washing machines, pianos and other heavy furniture. Cooking utensils and other small items will be accepted if crated, packed and plainly marked with the name and address of the owner. Only one name and address will be used by a given family.

4. Each family, and individual living alone, will be furnished transportation to the Reception Center. Private means of transportation will not be utilized. All instructions pertaining to the movement will be obtained at the Civil Control Station.

Go to the Civil Control Station at
1701 Van Ness Avenue, San Francisco, California,
between 8:00 a.m. and 5:00 p.m., Thursday, April 2, 1942,
or between 8:00 a.m. and 5:00 p.m., Friday, April 3, 1942,
to receive further instructions.

J. L. DeWITT
Lieutenant General, U. S. Army
Commanding

The Tolan Committee released its preliminary report a few hours after Roosevelt issued the order to implement the evacuation. The report generally acknowledged the need to remove Japanese Americans from the West Coast. The Tolan Committee strongly advised against imprisoning the ethnic Japanese for the duration of the war, however. Such a move, the report noted, would waste taxpayers' money and unnecessarily alienate thousands of people. It would also infringe on the rights of citizens, the report concluded:

"Serious constitutional questions are raised by the forced detention of citizens against whom no individual charges are lodged."

Just three days later, Congress passed a bill making it a federal crime to violate orders issued by a military officer under Executive Order Number 9066. Roosevelt quickly signed the bill, which became Public Law 503. Congress's law gave General DeWitt the authority he sought to punish civilians who disobeyed his orders. Under the law, violators would be subject to a $5,000 fine or a year in jail.

With the support of both branches of government, DeWitt stepped up preparations for the forced move of 110,000 Japanese Americans. Responsibility for moving civilians from their homes fell to the army's WCCA, but DeWitt did not want to saddle the army with the task of supervising the detainees once they had left the area. That job went to the WRA. The president named Milton S. Eisenhower director of the WRA and allotted $5.5 million for use in settling the Japanese Americans.

Eisenhower believed that most of the Japanese Americans should be allowed to live in government centers and work in the surrounding communities. He aimed to resettle the Japanese Americans in inland states. His goal was to allow the evacuees to live as normal a life as possible. The political winds did not favor Eisenhower's plan. The governors of the states chosen for the resettlement strongly resented the proposal. They refused to be a "dumping ground" for California's problems. If West Coast regions saw Japanese Americans as a menace, so, too, did those in the heartland. At a meeting with Eisenhower on the matter, the governors demanded that the evacuees be enclosed in guarded camps and kept under strict supervision. They also insisted that the Japanese-American detainees not be allowed to remain in their states or own land there after the war.

Without the governors' cooperation, Eisenhower realized he could not implement his plan. The "settlement camps" would become prisons, surrounded by barbed wire and overseen by armed guards. Eventually, 110,000 Japanese Americans, including nearly 70,000 U.S. citizens, would be moved to ten camps in undeveloped areas in the West. The detainees, half of whom were children, would live for up to four years there. California, Arizona, and Arkansas each had two camps: Tule Lake and Manzanar in California, Poston and Gila River in Arizona, and Jerome and Rohwer in Arkansas. Heart Mountain in Wyoming, Granada in Colorado, Minidoka in Idaho, and Topaz in Utah housed the remaining detainees.

The first large group of Japanese Americans reported voluntarily to the Manzanar assembly center in California's Owens Valley on March 22, 1942. The center would later become a permanent camp. Surrounded by the steep mountains of the Sierra Nevada and White-Inyo range, Manzanar was built on an abandoned farm and orchard. The desertlike environment made the site hot in the summer and cold in the winter. Thin pine boards covered with tarpaper offered meager protection from the weather.

Forced evacuaTIon BeGIns

Two days later, on March 24, DeWitt issued the first evacuation order, Civilian Exclusion Order No. 1. The order
banished all ethnic Japanese from Bainbridge Island in
Puget Sound, Washington. The people there had one week
to prepare for their removal to a temporary detention
center in Puyallup, near Seattle. Army officers informed
the forty-five affected families and registered them. The
families spent the next six days trying to pack the few
belongings they were allowed to take with them and selling
the rest. A military bus took them to Puyallup center,
where they were processed and assigned living quarters.

The center had been hurriedly constructed on the site
of a fairground and nearby parking lots. Officials called
Puyallup a "reception" center, but barbed wire and armed
military police greeted the families as they stepped down
from the bus onto the dry, dusty grounds. At Puyallup, as
at most of the centers, families lived together in barracks
or in converted horse stables. Wooden partitions separated the units into rooms that measured 20 feet by 20 feet
per family. A communal bathroom and a dining hall
served those in each set of buildings. The local newspaper
referred to the temporary buildings as "rabbit hutches":

> Four hutches to a row, six rooms to a hutch. Each
> room is about 20 feet square and separated from
> the next room by a partition that runs up part way
> to the roof. Each room is to house a Japanese
> family.

On March 27, DeWitt's third proclamation banned all
enemy aliens and ethnic Japanese from a long list of prohibited areas. It also required them to abide by a curfew
from 8 p.m. to 6 a.m. in Military Area No. 1. At all other
times, enemy aliens and "persons of Japanese ancestry"

MILTON S. EISENHOWER, BROTHER OF PRESIDENT DWIGHT D. EISENHOWER, STANDS IN FRONT OF A MAP OF THE WORLD IN THE 1960S. HE SERVED BRIEFLY AS THE FIRST DIRECTOR OF THE WAR RELOCATION AUTHORITY, IN CHARGE OF OVERSEEING THE INTERNMENT OF JAPANESE AMERICANS DURING WORLD WAR II. EISENHOWER BELIEVED THAT THE DETAINEES SHOULD BE FREE TO WORK IN SURROUNDING COMMUNITIES, BUT HIS VIEWS WERE NOT POLITICALLY POPULAR AND HE WAS SOON REPLACED AS WRA DIRECTOR.

A SIGN POSTED IN THE WINDOW OF THIS LOS ANGELES STORE IN APRIL 1942 BIDS FAREWELL TO CUSTOMERS. THE OWNERS WERE AMONG THE THOUSANDS OF WEST COAST JAPANESE AMERICANS FORCED TO ABANDON THEIR HOMES AND BUSINESSES AND LIVE IN INTERNMENT CAMPS DURING WORLD WAR II.

in the area could only be at work, at home, or within five miles of their homes. Two days later, DeWitt ended voluntary evacuation altogether. Ethnic Japanese could no longer leave Military Area No. 1 until ordered to do so.

After the Bainbridge Island evacuation, DeWitt issued another 107 civilian exclusion orders to move Japanese Americans from their homes on the West Coast. Each group of one thousand or so had six days to prepare for the move after being notified of the order. Under Civilian Restriction Order No. 1, issued on May 19, it became a crime for detainees to leave detention centers where they were being held.

By June 2, 1942, the military had moved all ethnic Japanese from Military Area 1 to assembly centers. The evacuation orders applied to anyone with one-sixteenth or more of Japanese blood—even Japanese babies adopted by Caucasian parents. Only those too ill to travel were left behind in army custody.

Many of the assembly centers had not yet been completed when the first detainees arrived. They helped construct the temporary camps. Disorganized and dirty, the assembly centers provided only the very basics of life. Thousands of people crowded into tiny cell-like rooms in converted stalls and shabbily constructed buildings. Remarkably, few incidents of rebellion occurred. Most people believed that by obeying military orders they would prove their loyalty to America.

Once Area 1 had been evacuated, DeWitt turned his attention to Military Area 2, in the eastern section of the West Coast states. Several thousand ethnic Japanese had moved to this area to comply with the ban in force in Area 1. Now they, along with other residents of the eastern areas, were taken directly to detention centers.

The army completed the entire evacuation in about

four months. By the first week in August, DeWitt told the press that almost 120,000 Japanese Americans had been removed from the West Coast. Transfers from assembly centers to camps took longer. Because of delays in construction, the permanent camps did not accept the last of the detainees until October 30. For the most part, conditions at the camps were not much better than in the assembly centers.

Forced to abandon businesses, homes, and careers, Japanese Americans suffered severe economic hardship. With such short notice, they had little time to make arrangements for the property left behind. Army regulations allowed each family to take only items they could carry with them. These items included sheets and blankets, toiletries, clothes, and eating utensils. Some asked friends and neighbors to hold their belongings or sell them and send them the money. Farmers left ripening crops in the hands of employees with instructions to harvest the produce and send on a share of the profits. In most cases, the evacuees received neither property nor money. A Congressional study conducted in 1983 estimated that Japanese Americans lost between $810 million and $2 billion in property and income due to the evacuation and detention (based on 1983 dollars). Following the war, Japanese Americans filed 26,568 claims totaling $148 million after Congress passed the Japanese American Evacuation Claims Act in 1948. The claims represented only a fraction of the economic losses and did not include personal sacrifices, career setbacks, psychological damages, and other intangible losses endured by those held in the camps.

Three
CITIZENS GO TO COURT

LIKE OTHER YOUNG AMERICAN MEN of the time, Fred Korematsu registered for the draft after graduating from high school. Stomach ulcers prevented him from being accepted into military service. He attended Los Angeles Junior College, studying chemistry and working to support himself. When he ran out of money after only a month, he dropped out of school and joined his father in the family's nursery business in Oakland, California. Later he studied welding and eventually found part-time work at shipyards in northern California. He began dating a young woman of Italian heritage who lived in the area. After the attack on Pearl Harbor, the union that represented the shipyard's welders expelled members of Japanese heritage. That meant Korematsu could no longer work at the shipyard. He had to depend on freelance welding jobs with small-time contractors.

On March 2, 1942, General DeWitt declared Almeida County, where the Korematsus lived, under military control. Korematsu and his girlfriend, who had recently become engaged, planned to move to the Midwest after saving enough money for the trip. While working toward that goal, Korematsu saw an advertisement by a doctor who performed plastic surgery. At his fiancée's suggestion, he decided to undergo surgery to change his looks and avoid anti-Japanese violence. In mid-March, the doctor operated on his eyelids and nose. Korematsu also changed his name to Clyde Sarah in an attempt to hide his Japanese heritage. The surgery failed to hide his Japanese features. On May 9, the general issued Exclusion Order No. 34 requiring Japanese Americans to leave the area and relocate to a government-run camp. Forced to abandon their home and their business, the Korematsu family joined other Japanese Americans at the Tanforan assembly center, outside San Francisco, California. Later they were taken to a guarded prison camp in the Utah desert.

Fred Korematsu decided not to go to the assembly center with his parents and three brothers. He told his family he planned to move to Nebraska. Instead he stayed in Oakland and got a job in Berkeley. The area lay within Military Area No. 1, which DeWitt had declared off-limits to those of Japanese descent.

On May 30, 1942, police arrested Korematsu as he and his fiancée walked down the streets of San Leandro, California. Korematsu told police his name was Clyde Sarah and showed them his draft card, which had been changed to reflect his new name. The change had been made by painting over his real name with ink correction fluid. Police quickly discovered the deception. Other aspects of Korematsu's story were also suspect. He told police he was Spanish Hawaiian and had been born in Las Vegas, but police soon learned that the young man in custody could neither speak nor understand Spanish. He eventually confessed his real name and the fact that he was of Japanese ancestry.

The Federal Bureau of Investigation soon took over his case. When the agents questioned him further, the young man told them the truth. Love and his desire to marry his girlfriend had led him to hide his Japanese heritage and ignore the order to go to the assembly center, he said. Korematsu believed that the local pharmacist had recognized him when he went into the store and had reported him to the police.

Five Test Cases

During this time, the Northern California chapter of the American Civil Liberties Union (ACLU) had been looking for a plaintiff to challenge the legality of DeWitt's evacuation order and the subsequent relocation of Japanese Americans. A plaintiff is the person on whose behalf a lawsuit is filed. Courts will not hear cases based solely on abstract questions. In order to get a court hearing, lawyers must file suit in the name of a plaintiff who contends a particular law or action has unjustly harmed him or her.

The day after Korematsu's arrest, the local newspaper ran an article about the incident headlined "Jap Spy Arrested in San Leandro." The story brought ACLU director Ernest Besig to Korematsu's cell at the San Francisco County Jail, where he was being held after his arrest. Would the young man consider challenging the law? Besig asked. Korematsu said he would.

Korematsu had not openly defied the authorities, nor had he intended to test the law. Shy and reserved, he had tried not to get caught. Love, not politics, had been his motivation in disobeying the relocation order. Nevertheless, once the police arrested him, he willingly agreed to play his part in the ACLU challenge. "I didn't feel guilty because I didn't do anything wrong," Korematsu said years later. "Every day in school we said the pledge to the flag, 'with liberty and justice for all,' and I believed all that. I was an American citizen and I had as many rights as anyone else."

Besig paid Korematsu's bail of $5,000, but armed soldiers outside the jail refused to let the young man go free. Shortly after Korematsu's meeting with Besig, authorities sent him to the Tanforan assembly center. There he joined his parents and brothers. Many of the Japanese Americans at the center advised against court action. They wanted to prove their patriotism by not protesting the military's actions. Korematsu, however, remained firm in his determination to pursue the case.

Korematsu never saw his girlfriend again after his arrest. When FBI agents questioned her about him, she told them she had ended the relationship.

As Korematsu prepared for trial, two other plaintiffs filed suits related to the Japanese-American situation. Minoru Yasui and Gordon Hirabayashi had filed separate suits challenging the legality of the curfew and the relocation order imposed on Japanese-American citizens.

Yasui, an American-born citizen from Oregon, was an officer in the U.S. army reserves. After earning his law degree, he had worked for the Japanese consulate in Chicago. As soon as he heard of the Japanese attack on Pearl Harbor, he resigned from the post and volunteered for military service. Yasui intentionally challenged DeWitt's order, which he considered unconstitutional, by going to a local police station after curfew and demanding to be arrested.

"The thing that struck me immediately was that

MINORU YASUI WAS AN AMERICAN-BORN CITIZEN FROM OREGON WHO WAS AN OFFICER IN THE U.S. ARMY RESERVES. HE WAS ONE OF THREE JAPANESE-AMERICAN CITIZENS TO CHALLENGE MILITARY ORDERS DIRECTED AGAINST WEST COAST RESIDENTS OF JAPANESE HERITAGE.

the military was ordering the civilian to do something," recalled Yasui years later. "In my opinion, that's the way dictatorships are formed. And if I, as an American citizen stood still for this, I would be derogating the rights of all citizens."

Hirabayashi, a senior at the University of Washington, challenged the order to go to a relocation center. His parents had already gone to the center, but unlike his parents, Hirabayashi was an American citizen, born in the United States. "We (citizens) had Constitutional rights," he said later. "I didn't think anything could happen to us. We had a rude awakening."

GORDON HIRABAYASHI, WHO AS A TWENTY-FOUR-YEAR-OLD COLLEGE STUDENT, CHALLENGED THE ORDER TO GO TO A RELOCATION CENTER. HIS CONVICTION FOR DISOBEYING A MILITARY ORDER WAS LATER UPHELD BY THE U.S. SUPREME COURT.

When the bus arrived to take Hirabayashi to the center, he decided to protest the evacuation order. "I thought, 'I'm not going to allow my citizenship to be usurped without my protest. I'm going to stand up for my rights.' Immediately I knew I couldn't board the bus."

He reported to the FBI instead. Agents arrested him and charged him with violating DeWitt's order.

San Francisco lawyer James Purcell recruited Mitsuye Endo to test the legality of the government's internment camps. She was one of hundreds of state workers of Japanese heritage who had been fired from their jobs after President Roosevelt issued his proclamation. Her case, first filed in San Francisco federal district court on July 12,

1942, contended that the army had unlawfully detained her at the assembly center, and later in a relocation camp. She would spend the next two years behind barbed wire while Purcell, working without fee, argued her case. A fifth case was filed by the ACLU in Los Angeles on behalf of Ernest and Toki Wakayama. The couple had been held at the Santa Anita Assembly Center near Los Angeles since DeWitt's order in May. A postal worker and veteran of World War I, Ernest Wakayama fiercely resented such treatment. Like the *Endo* case, the *Wakayama* suit argued that the plaintiffs should be released because the army had illegally imprisoned them. The case would later be dropped after Ernest Wakayama renounced his American citizenship and asked to become a Japanese citizen in February 1943.

GUILTY as charged

Korematsu's lawyers, Wayne Collins and Clarence E. Rust, answered the charges against their client in the U.S. District Court of the Northern District of California. Their written response to the government's charges, filed on June 20, 1942, listed a string of claims that Roosevelt's and DeWitt's orders violated Korematsu's constitutional rights. The strongest arguments centered on the claim that Korematsu had been deprived of the right to a hearing and of the right to equal protection of the laws.

Collins argued for the defense during a hearing on August 31, 1942, on whether to dismiss the charges against Korematsu. Deputy U.S. Attorney Alfonso Zirpoli presented the government's arguments in the case. Judge Martin I. Welsh presided. President Roosevelt had appointed Welsh to the bench in 1939. The first judge to sit permanently in Sacramento, Welsh was a member of the anti-immigrant Native Sons of the Golden West. The organization had filed suit in federal court earlier that year to strip the children of Japanese immigrants of their U.S. citizenship. That case had been dismissed in July 1942. The following year the group would push for a constitutional amendment to block Japanese Americans born in the United States from being citizens.

It took Judge Welsh only twenty-eight words to turn down Korematsu's request for dismissal. He did not address any of the constitutional issues discussed in the *Korematsu* brief. The judge scheduled a new hearing, this time examining the charges against Korematsu, for September 8, 1942.

Judge Adolphus F. St. Sure oversaw the new hearing. Both sides chose to have the case decided by the judge rather than by a jury. The state's prosecutor, Zirpoli, relied on the testimony of FBI agent Oliver Mansfield to make his case against Korematsu. The agent told the court of Korematsu's confession and his efforts to conceal his identity by changing his name and his looks. Since his client had already admitted that he had taken those actions, Collins again focused on constitutional issues. Even if Korematsu had acted to avoid DeWitt's order, Collins argued, the order itself violated Korematsu's constitutional rights and the charges should be dismissed. The judge denied Collins's request for dismissal.

Called to the stand, Korematsu testified that he had taken the actions he was accused of. In further testimony, however, he showed himself to be an earnest young man who had worked hard to put himself through school and who considered himself an American without ties to Japan. Judge St. Sure found Korematsu guilty as charged and gave him five years of probation. In most cases when probation is given, the judge first sentences the defendant to pay a fine or to serve time in jail. Defendants who fulfill the terms of probation are released from the sentence; those who do not meet the requirements of probation must pay fines or go to jail or both. The judge in Korematsu's case, apparently impressed by the defendant's honesty, imposed no sentence at all on the young man. That act would later prove to be a problem when Korematsu's lawyers tried to appeal the case.

The judge set bail, and the ACLU agreed to cover the fees so that Korematsu could remain free during the appeal process. Instead, the military police took him into custody and eventually sent him to the Tanforan assembly center. Korematsu later recalled that the judge had set him free, but the military policeman "pulled a gun on me and said he's not going to let me go." The courtroom confrontation—between the judge and the military police—ended when the judge backed down and allowed Korematsu to be led away.

TWO TRIALS, TWO GUILTY VERDICTS

After five months in the King County, Washington, jail, Gordon Hirabayashi presented his case before the U.S. District Court in Seattle on October 20, 1942. The trial lasted one day. The government had brought Hirabayashi's parents from the Tule Lake camp to testify. Both his mother and his father had been put in jail for ten days waiting for the trial to begin. Judge Lloyd Black told the jury that DeWitt's curfew and evacuation order were "valid and enforceable." After deliberating the case for only ten minutes, the jury found Hirabayashi guilty of violating a curfew and refusing to evacuate a military area.

The following day, Black gave Hirabayashi a ninety-day sentence on both counts, to be served concurrently. Hirabayashi and his lawyers agreed to the concurrent sentence, not realizing that the U.S. Supreme Court would use that to avoid ruling on the major issue of evacuation. While his lawyers appealed the conviction, Hirabayashi stayed in jail until a Quaker group arranged for him to work in Spokane, Washington, outside the evacuation zone.

In November, Minoru Yasui appeared before Oregon District Court Judge James Fee to answer the charges against him. Fee found Yasui guilty of violating DeWitt's curfew and sentenced him to one year in jail and a $5,000 fine. The judge ruled that the Constitution protected citizens from laws based on color or race. Aliens, however, had no such guarantees, according to the judge. The curfew applied to Yasui, Fee said, because the young man was not a citizen. Yasui had been born and raised in the United States, had voted, and had received a commission as second lieutenant in the U.S. Officers Reserve Corps. Nevertheless, the judge contended that Yasui had "chosen" to be a citizen of Japan. Yasui's parents were Japanese, which automatically gave Yasui dual citizenship. According to Judge Fee, Yasui made his choice to become a citizen of Japan when he went to work for the Consulate General of Japan at Chicago. Yasui had resigned from his position immediately after the Pearl Harbor attack, but that carried no weight with the judge. Yasui's lawyers appealed the decision to the circuit court.

APPEALING THE CASES

Korematsu's lawyers also prepared to appeal their client's case to a higher court. Problems arose, however, over the judge's failure to sentence Korematsu. Since the judge had imposed no sentence, the government argued, Korematsu had nothing to appeal. At a December 23 hearing, Collins tried to persuade St. Sure to sentence Korematsu to a short stay in jail, then suspend the sentence. That way, he explained, the case could proceed to the appeals court without question. The judge refused to take further action.

Nevertheless, on Friday, February 19, 1943, Collins

joined lawyers for Hirabayashi and Yasui at a hearing before the full seven-member U.S. Circuit Court of Appeals for the Ninth Circuit. On that date a year before, President Roosevelt had issued Executive Order 9066, the document that had led to the cases now under consideration.

A case heard immediately before the three appeals highlighted the anti-Japanese sentiment of the day. The case involved an attempt by white voters in California to bar Japanese-American citizens from voting. The group's lawyer, Ulysses S. Webb, contended that the Constitution had been written to set up "a government of, for and by white people." The racial traits of Japanese Americans, he continued, included "dishonesty, deceit and hypocrisy." The court quickly dismissed the case, but the poisonous comments of the attorney lingered in the courtroom.

Collins led off the appeals with many of the same arguments he had used before. He contended that the court had the power to review military orders and reiterated his claims that DeWitt's orders had violated the Constitution.

Frank Walters, arguing on behalf of Hirabayashi, focused on the equal protection clause of the Fifth Amendment. He claimed that the government was not treating Japanese-American citizens equally with other citizens when it excluded them based solely on their race. "If these things can be done to one minority group, such as the Japanese, they can be done to other minority groups, merely because they happen to be Chinese, or Negroes, or Jews or Catholics," he told the court.

Walters also argued that DeWitt had violated the Constitution when he issued the evacuation orders. Only Congress had such powers, he contended.

Observers from the ACLU and others criticized the performances of both lawyers. They believed Collins had weakened his case by introducing too many arguments.

Walters, on the other hand, had ignored crucial points—failing to dispute the military's claim that the evacuation was necessary, for one—in making his case.

The third case, involving Yasui's curfew violation, came before the judge next. Yasui's lawyer, Earl Bernard, argued that his client was a citizen and that the lower court judge had already ruled the government's curfew violated citizens' rights.

The government lawyers conceded that Yasui was indeed an American citizen, but they disputed Judge Fee's ruling that the curfew was unconstitutional. In making his case for the government, Deputy U.S. Attorney Zirpoli told the court that the military had to enforce the curfew and the evacuation to ensure national security. The evacuation, he argued, served two purposes: to prevent sabotage by Japanese Americans and to protect the Asian population from hostile neighbors. He repeated DeWitt's claims that white military staff could not tell which Japanese were loyal citizens and which were not. But another government attorney, Edward Ennis, director of the Justice Department's Alien Enemy Control Unit, conceded that there had not been even one case of espionage or harm to the nation caused by a Japanese American. Even so, the government argued, the Japanese Americans could have organized a campaign to support the enemy.

The hearing stretched to Saturday as the lawyers made their lengthy arguments in the three cases. While they waited for a ruling on their cases, Korematsu and Yasui lived in camps with other Japanese Americans. Barbed wire and armed guards prevented them from leaving. Hirabayashi remained in jail.

four
U.S. SUPREME COURT
ROUND I

FIVE WEEKS AFTER THE HEARING, on March 27,
1943, the Circuit Court of Appeals issued its response.
Instead of ruling on the appeals, the court asked the
Supreme Court to settle the constitutional questions
raised during the hearing. This process, called certification, allows a case to pass to the high court without further
delay, provided the Supreme Court justices agree to hear
the case.

Justice Department lawyers had urged the lower court
to seek certification in the appeals cases. The majority of
the court went along with the push for a quick review of the
issues by the Supreme Court. Judge William Denman,
however, wrote a strong rebuke. In his dissenting
opinion, Denman objected to the rush to take the decision
out of the hands of the lower court, which he believed was
better equipped to judge the effects of the military orders.
His opinion, however, rambled on for three thousand
words and criticized both sides as well as the army for
unrelated misdeeds. The other judges distanced themselves from Denman's comments.

On April 5, Chief Justice Harlan Fiske Stone announced
that the Supreme Court would review all three appeals
cases. In Korematsu's suit, however, the Court would decide
only whether the case could be appealed, since the judge

had never sentenced the defendant. The other two cases, closely tied to Korematsu's, would be argued on the issues. Oral arguments were scheduled for May 10, in time for the justices to decide the cases before they adjourned for the term in June.

The imminent deadline caught the lawyers by surprise. They had thought the cases would travel the usual route through the courts before reaching the Supreme Court. That process took months, sometimes years, to complete. Each year hundreds of petitioners seek review of their cases by the Supreme Court. In the mid–1940s, the Court's docket contained almost 1,500 cases waiting for action. Today that number has grown to more than 9,000. Each term the Court hears oral arguments in about 100 cases. To win a spot on the Court's schedule, a case must deal with one of three issues:

1. a dispute between states and the federal government or between two or more states;
2. a federal question that has been appealed from a state court; or
3. an appeal from a federal appeals court.

In most cases, the appellant, or petitioner—the person appealing the case—asks the Court for a hearing. The request is made by filing a petition for a *writ of certiorari*. Few of these cases are ever heard. Most are rejected because they do not meet the requirements for a Supreme Court case, the Court has already dealt with the issue, or the justices simply vote against hearing the case. Four justices must vote to consider a case for it to win a hearing. In the Japanese-American cases, the petitioners did not need to file a petition since the lower court requested that the Court review the cases.

With the Court hearing just six weeks away, lawyers on both sides spent long hours organizing their briefs and planning oral presentations. Preparing the briefs for the case proved to be far more difficult than winning Court review. For months, since the first Japanese-American case headed for appeal in the fall of 1942, the lawyers on both sides had wrangled among themselves. On the government side, lawyers in the Department of Justice tangled with Department of War officials. Long before the cases came to court, members of the Justice Department had urged the administration to protect the rights of those interned in the camps. Those representing the Department of War and the U.S. Army took a much harder stance against Japanese-American rights. They believed that civilian courts did not have the authority to review General John DeWitt's military decisions.

In heated debates over the issues, both sides presented their views to Solicitor General Charles Fahy. The solicitor general holds the number two position in the Justice Department (behind the attorney general). The person serving in that post is the department's chief trial lawyer and argues cases involving the U.S. government before the Supreme Court. Fahy would present the government's side to the Supreme Court in all three of the Japanese-American cases.

While working on the *Hirabayashi* brief, Edward Ennis of the Justice Department discovered reports by naval intelligence officer Lt. Commander Kenneth Ringle. After Pearl Harbor, Ringle had investigated West Coast Japanese Americans extensively. He reported to DeWitt and others in the administration that only a small number of Japanese Americans might be disloyal. Based on that, he recommended evacuating ten thousand people at the most rather than the mass removal favored by DeWitt.

Ennis advised Fahy that he should tell the Supreme Court of Ringle's report. "I think we should consider very carefully whether we do not have a duty to advise the Court of the existence of the Ringle memorandum and of the fact that this represents the view of the Office of Naval Intelligence," Ennis wrote Fahy. "It occurs to me that any other course of conduct might approximate the suppression of evidence."

If Fahy revealed the report, however, it would undermine DeWitt's claim that the evacuation was militarily necessary. In the end Fahy chose not to include the Ringle report in the material submitted to the Court.

Years later, lawyers for the Japanese Americans would use Fahy's decision—an error before the Court—to clear their clients' names. But in 1943, the legal teams representing the four Japanese Americans had no inkling that the Ringle report existed. Neither did the members of the U.S. Supreme Court.

For the Appellants

On the appellants' side, the local branch and the national board of the ACLU disagreed on how to present the cases. By the 1940s, the ACLU had established itself as the national voice for protecting civil rights. Its prominence attracted some of the best legal experts in the country. With funds provided by wealthy supporters and a multitude of other donors, the ACLU had the money and expertise that Supreme Court challenges required. The ACLU had long been a champion of President Roosevelt and the policies of the New Deal. Members of the national organization were reluctant to challenge the power of the president to issue the exclusion order. Though they supported efforts to preserve the civil rights of Japanese Americans who suffered the consequences of the order,

THrouGH THe couRT sYsTem

FirsT sTop: sTaTe couRT

Almost all cases (about 95 percent) start in state courts. Depending on the state, these courts go by various names, depending on the state in which they operate: circuit, district, municipal, county, or superior courts. The case is tried and decided by a judge, a panel of judges, or a jury. The side that loses can then appeal to the next level.

FirsT sTop: FeDeraL couRT

U.S. DISTRICT COURT—About 5 percent of cases begin their journey in federal court. Most of these cases concern federal laws, the U.S. Constitution, or disputes that involve two or more states. They are heard in one of the ninety-four U.S. District Courts in the nation.

U.S. COURT OF INTERNATIONAL TRADE—Federal court cases involving international trade appear in the U.S. Court of International Trade.

U.S. CLAIMS COURT—The U.S. Claims Court hears federal cases that involve more than $10,000, Indian claims, and some disputes with government contractors.

The loser in federal court can appeal to the next level.

APPeaLs: sTaTe cases

Forty states have appeals courts that hear cases that have come from the state courts. In states without an appeals court, the case goes directly to the state supreme court.

APPeaLs: FeDeraL cases

U.S. CIRCUIT COURT—Cases appealed from U.S. District Courts go to U.S. Circuit Courts of Appeals. There are twelve circuit courts that handle cases from throughout the nation. Each district court and every state and territory are assigned to one of the twelve circuits. Appeals in a few state cases—those that deal with rights guaranteed by the U.S. Constitution—are also heard in this court.

U.S. COURT OF APPEALS—Cases appealed from the U.S. Court of International Trade and the U.S. Claims Court are heard by the U.S. Court of Appeals for the Federal Circuit. Among the cases heard in this court are those involving patents and minor claims against the federal government.

Further Appeals: State Supreme Court
Cases appealed from state appeals courts go to the highest courts in the state—usually called supreme court. In New York, the state's highest court is called the court of appeals. Most state cases do not go beyond this point.

Final Appeals: U.S. Supreme Court
The U.S. Supreme Court is the highest court in the country. Its decision on a case is the final word. The Court decides issues that can affect every person in the nation. It has decided cases on slavery, abortion, school segregation, and many other important issues. The Court selects the cases it will hear—usually around one hundred each year. Four of the nine justices must vote to consider a case in order for it to be heard. Almost all cases have been appealed from the lower courts (either state or federal).

Most people seeking a decision from the Court submit a petition for *certiorari*. *Certiorari* means that the case will be moved from a lower court to a higher court for review. The Court receives more than nine thousand of these requests annually. The petition outlines the case and gives reasons why the Court should review it.

In rare cases, for example *New York Times* v. *United States*, an issue must be decided immediately. When such a case is of national importance, the Court allows it to bypass the usual lower court system and hears the case directly.

To win a spot on the Court's docket, a case must fall within one of the following categories:

- Disputes between states and the federal government or between two or more states. The Court also reviews cases involving ambassadors, consuls, and foreign ministers.

- Appeals from a state court that has ruled on a federal question.

- Appeals from federal appeals courts (about two-thirds of all requests fall into this category).

they did not want to be viewed during war as being soft on the nation's enemies.

Instead of attacking Roosevelt, the national board focused its arguments on Congress and DeWitt. In the *Hirabayashi* brief, the ACLU team argued that Public Law 503 illegally gave the military unlimited power to set up restricted zones and to control civilians living inside those zones. ACLU lawyer A. L. Wirin made similar arguments in the Minoru Yasui case.

Under the rules of the Court, groups or people who are not directly involved in a lawsuit but who believe the case may affect them in some way may file briefs on either side of a question. These briefs are called *amicus curiae*, from the Latin phrase meaning "friend of the court." The parties in the suit or the court must approve the submission of such briefs. Government agencies—such as the United States or the individual states—do not need such permission. Often *amicus curiae* briefs contain analyses, information, or personal stories that add to the court's understanding of the issue under discussion. In rare cases of extreme national importance, the Court may ask lawyers presenting an *amicus curiae* brief to give oral arguments in the case.

The Northern California ACLU, headed by Ernest Besig, refused to go along with the national organization's approach. In the *Hirabayashi* case, the group filed a separate *amicus* brief, written by Collins, the lawyer representing Korematsu. In angry words, Collins berated DeWitt, attacked the president's actions in issuing his executive order, and demanded that the Court rule in Hirabayashi's favor.

The Japanese American Citizens League also filed an *amicus* brief on Hirabayashi's behalf. Reversing its position against supporting such suits, the JACL argued that

DeWitt had issued his orders not for necessary military reasons but because of racist attitudes. It cited several studies that showed that ethnic Japanese, like other immigrants, had adopted the American way of life. They were just as loyal as any other group, the brief argued. Another *amicus* brief, this one filed by the states of California, Washington, and Oregon, supported the government's side in the *Hirabayashi* case. In their brief, the lawyers presented arguments that reflected the hardline views of the military and the Department of War. Many of the arguments used in the brief came directly from General DeWitt's *Final Report* on the evacuation, which had not yet been released. DeWitt's report contained a lengthy list of suspicious behavior and activities by Japanese Americans. None of the examples, however, were based on fact. In fact, several government agencies, including the FBI, disputed DeWitt's assertions. Nevertheless, the states' brief repeated DeWitt's claims. It also noted that the "racial characteristics" of Japanese Americans tied them to the enemy nation of Japan. A similar point had been made in the *Final Report*.

LOYaLTY OaTH

As the lawyers prepared their briefs in the Japanese-American cases, administration officials battled over the fate of those incarcerated in the relocation camps. A number of students had been quietly released to attend colleges outside the military zones. Other detainees had left the camps to labor on farms and in other jobs desperate for workers.

With the war escalating, officials pondered the role the young Nisei should play in the military. After the attack on Pearl Harbor, the military had classified Japanese Americans who otherwise qualified for the draft as "enemy

Lieutenant General John L. DeWitt, left, confers with Mexican General Lazaro Cardenas on matters of defense on January 22, 1942. DeWitt later issued orders to exclude and then to evacuate all Japanese Americans from the West Coast.

MEMBERS OF THE 100TH BATTALION OF THE 442ND INFANTRY POSE FOR A
PHOTOGRAPHER ON JUNE 20, 1945, AFTER RECEIVING DECORATIONS FOR THEIR
SERVICE DURING WORLD WAR II. THE MILITARY DIVISION, MADE UP ENTIRELY
OF JAPANESE AMERICANS, BECAME THE MOST DECORATED UNIT OF THE WAR.
FRONT ROW, FROM LEFT: GEORGE H. SUNADA, TOSHIO FUKUDA, ISAO
SHIOZAKI, GEORGE S. IZUTA, SHIGEO TANABE, MASTANI MORIKUNI,
YOSHINORI ODA, AND KAZUO SENDA. BACK ROW, FROM LEFT: JITSUO SAIKI,
TSUTONU OGATA, ROY N. YAMADA, YUTAKA KUMUJE, MASAICHI TOWATA,
DONALD K. HAMADA, SHIGERU USHIJIMA, PAUL M. SHIMABUKURO, AND
RICHARD K. HAMADA.

aliens." Many who had already enlisted in the armed forces
were discharged. The restrictions were eased to allow Nisei
volunteers in Hawaii to form the 100th Infantry Battalion in
May 1942. The following January, President Roosevelt acti-
vated the 442nd Regimental Combat Team, a segregated
unit made up entirely of Nisei volunteers from Hawaii and
the mainland. The two teams joined forces in June 1944 and
eventually became the most decorated unit of World War II.

JACL's Mike Masaoka proposed that Nisei men in the camps be allowed to volunteer to serve as U.S. soldiers to prove their loyalty. The WRA supported the idea. Under the proposal, soldiers who completed their tour of duty would be allowed to return to their homes on the West Coast. The plan fit well with WRA's recommendation that loyal camp residents gradually be permitted to go home.

General DeWitt argued vehemently against the return of any Japanese Americans to the West Coast. Even the Nisei soldiers' valiant military service did not persuade him that they should be allowed to go back to their West Coast communities. DeWitt said such a move would weaken the government's arguments in the pending Supreme Court cases. All along, the army had contended that it could not judge the loyalty of ethnic Japanese. If loyalty tests were used now, DeWitt noted, opponents of the evacuation would contend that the army could have followed the same procedure before removal of Japanese Americans from the West Coast. That would have eliminated the need for a mass evacuation. DeWitt insisted that those at the camps should be held there until the war ended.

WRA officials, however, argued that a plan to release loyal Japanese Americans would make the government's position more credible. It would be easier to defend the original actions, they said, if the army made an effort to protect the rights of loyal citizens. Such an approach, they said, made sense because recent U.S. victories had reduced the threat of a West Coast invasion.

DeWitt reluctantly agreed to the plan to allow Nisei at the camps to sign up for military service. To determine those eligible and test the loyalty of other detainees, the WRA circulated a form to all camp residents who were at least seventeen years old. The form, called the Loyalty Questionnaire, contained two key questions:

No. 27. Are you willing to serve in the Armed forces of the United States on combat duty wherever ordered?

No. 28. Will you swear unqualified allegiance to the United States of America and faithfully defend the United States from any or all attack by foreign or domestic forces, and forswear any form of allegiance or obedience to the Japanese emperor, to any other foreign government, power or organization?

The questionnaire caused immediate turmoil in the camps. Question 27 seemed to imply that everyone should be willing to serve in the army if they were loyal Americans. But why should those who had been deprived of their rights as citizens be expected to fight for the country that had treated them badly? Women, old men, and those resentful over their unjust imprisonment hesitated to pledge that they would serve in the army and fight in combat. As George Takei, the Japanese-American actor who played Mr. Sulu on the television series *Star Trek*, noted in his autobiography: "The substance of American citizenship—most vitally, freedom and justice—was torn away from us, but now we were not to be denied the responsibility of citizenship. Japanese Americans had the right to be killed for a country that had humiliated them, stripped them of property and dignity and placed them behind barbed wire."

Question 28 posed another problem. Many regarded it as a trick question. If they answered yes, they would be admitting that they had once had allegiance to Japan. If they answered no, they would be rejecting allegiance to the United States. For the Issei, who could not by law become U.S. citizens, the question demanded that they agree to be "people without a country." Those who followed the Shinto faith believed the Japanese emperor was God. To answer yes to Question 28 would be to abandon their religion.

Even so, all but 10 percent of the detainees answered yes to both questions. The fact that about 7,600 Japanese Americans did not wholeheartedly agree, however, fueled DeWitt's campaign to keep the detainees out of the West Coast. Those who answered no or refused to fill out the loyalty form became known as the No-No group. Many of them lived at the Tule Lake camp, where relations with authorities were particularly strained. Secretary of War Stimson ordered that dissenters in all the camps be separated from the rest of the detainees and shipped to Tule Lake. Before the war ended, several hundred of these protesters would renounce their American citizenship and become Japanese citizens. Some, disgusted by their treatment in America, went to live in Japan after the war.

Despite being held against their will in armed camps, most detainees continued to support their homeland. In February 1944, when notices went out to all Nisei men of draft age, approximately 1,200 Japanese Americans in the camps signed up to serve with the Nisei combat unit. In one of the ironies of the war, Nisei soldiers were among the first to liberate starving Jewish prisoners from Dachau, the concentration camp where Germans tortured and killed thousands. Though conditions were far more barbaric there, the barbed wire and gun towers of Dachau resembled those at the camps where the soldiers' families were imprisoned back home in their native land of America.

Using the results of the questionnaire, the WRA granted requests from about 16,000 detainees in 1943 to leave the camps and settle outside the West Coast. Those released had to show that they could support themselves and that the community would accept them. Church groups and others assisted in relocating those leaving the camps. Many still met with hostility in their new homes, however. New York City Mayor Fiorello LaGuardia complained about the influx of Japanese Americans to his city. He raised the often-repeated point that if the Japanese Americans were too dangerous for the West Coast, why should the East Coast accept them.

Dillon Myer, appointed in 1942 to replace Eisenhower as head of the WRA, hoped that a U.S. Supreme Court decision against detention would help speed the release of Japanese Americans. The American public, he believed, would be less likely to resist a Court ruling than an action ordered by the WRA:

> This is one case where I strongly believe that it is more desirable to have the change made as a result of a Court decision than a result of unforced administrative action.

The Court would soon rule on the cases presented by Japanese Americans. Its decisions, however, would neither resolve the issues raised by detention nor lift the restrictions imposed by DeWitt, as Myer hoped.

Arguing Their case

After a hectic six weeks preparing their cases, the lawyers for the Japanese Americans gathered at the U.S. Supreme Court on May 10, 1943, for oral arguments.

Even for experienced legal experts, arguing a case before the Supreme Court can be intimidating. The building itself, with the motto "Equal Justice Under Law" carved above massive marble columns, is awe-inspiring. Inside the courtroom where turning points in the nation's history have been decided, the nine justices in their black robes preside. Seated in black leather chairs on a raised platform, they look down on the proceedings. Behind them, red velvet drapes separate the room from the justices' private chambers. Twenty-four columns of Italian marble encircle the room.

The lawyers in the case sit facing the justices, a raised mahogany bench separating them from the Court. Hanging from the 44-foot-high ceiling, a large clock informs them of the time. Lawyers who argue before the Supreme Court have thirty minutes to make their case. Justices may extend that time with additional questions, but a lawyer who goes over the allotted time without the Court's blessing may look up to see nine pairs of eyes glaring down at him or her.

That morning, the nine justices solemnly entered the courtroom, following the ritual established by previous Courts. First to appear from behind the red drapes was Chief Justice Stone. The associate justices followed him in order of their years on the Court: Owen J. Roberts, Hugo L. Black, Stanley F. Reed, Felix Frankfurter, William O. Douglas, Frank Murphy, Robert H. Jackson, and finally newcomer Wiley B. Rutledge, who had taken his seat on the bench just three months before.

On the surface, the membership of the U.S. Supreme Court in the spring of 1943 did not bode well for the lawyers arguing on behalf of the Japanese-American clients. Of the nine justices, seven had been appointed to the Court by Franklin D. Roosevelt, the man who had issued Executive Order No. 9066. All seven had expressed strong support for the president's ambitious social programs. Only Chief Justice Stone and Justice Roberts had been named to the Court by someone other than Roosevelt. And the president had elevated Stone, a Republican, to the chief justice post in 1941. Stone had supported the president in a number of Court cases that had challenged Roosevelt's New Deal programs. Roberts, the associate justice who had served the longest, had headed the committee that had investigated the Pearl Harbor attack. The committee's report had suggested that Japanese-American spies had helped the enemy, and Roberts himself had told members of the Roosevelt administration that ethnic Japanese posed a threat.

May 10, 1943, was a busy Monday at the nation's highest court. Justices announced decisions in two other cases and read the opinions to those attending the session. After the readings, lawyers in four separate cases presented oral arguments. It was late afternoon before arguments in the Japanese-American cases began.

FIRST UP: HIRABAYASHI

The Court focused first on *Hirabayashi* v. *United States*. Frank Walters opened the arguments for Gordon Hirabayashi. None of the Japanese Americans at the heart of the three cases attended the hearing. Walters gave a brief rundown of the facts of the case. Justice Jackson interrupted Walters's discussion to ask if he considered DeWitt's orders to be *bills of attainder*. The phrase refers to an act by Congress that punishes a particular person or group without the benefit of a trial. Article 1 of the U.S. Constitution prohibits such action.

Walters readily agreed that the orders were bills of attainder. In followup questions, however, Jackson seemed to be saying that such a claim unwisely questioned military power during a war.

In the time remaining, attorney Harold Evans made the final arguments in Hirabayashi's defense. He focused on what he saw as the failings of Congress's Public Law 503. The law, he argued, was too vague. The U.S. Constitution put Congress, not the military, in charge of civilians, Evans noted. Under the American form of government, the military is allowed to control civilians only when they are in an area under attack or if Congress specifically orders the military to take certain actions. Public Law 503 contained no such specific orders. Congress had approved a fine and jail time for anyone who entered, remained in, left, or committed "any act" that violated restrictions set up by the military in military zones. Nowhere in the law did Congress refer to Japanese Americans or specifically authorize the military to remove them from the West Coast and hold them in guarded prison camps. General DeWitt far exceeded his authority, Evans told the Court, when he issued his orders.

In keeping with the ACLU's pledge not to attack Roosevelt, Evans did not question the power of the president to issue his executive order. Instead, he relied on an earlier case, *ex parte Milligan*, to make his case. The 1866 case involved an Indiana man, Lambdin Milligan. He had been arrested as a Confederate sympathizer and sentenced by a military tribunal to hang. In 1863 President Abraham Lincoln, with Congress's approval, had declared the entire country under martial law during the Civil War. Prosecutors argued that Lincoln's action gave military officials the power to punish Milligan. The Supreme Court disagreed. Martial law, the Court stated in its decision freeing Milligan, could only apply to areas where war was actually being fought.

Martial law cannot arise from a threatened invasion. The necessity must be actual and present; the invasion real, such as effectually closes the courts and deposes the civil administration.

The Court noted that Indiana, where Milligan lived, was not under direct attack and that civilian authorities there remained firmly in control. Likewise, Evans argued, the entire West Coast in 1942 did not fall under the Constitution's definition of a war zone. California, Hirabayashi's home, had not been invaded, Evans pointed out. It was 2,400 miles from Hawaii, where the attack on Pearl Harbor had occurred. The state's civilian courts and police departments continued to operate.

A barrage of questions and comments from the justices followed. Wasn't it up to the military to determine whether California was in imminent danger, Douglas wanted to know. No, Evans said, noting that there was no evidence to suggest an invasion would occur. Other justices raised questions about limits on the president's war powers and whether the *Milligan* ruling applied to wartime in the mid-twentieth century. Evans had no time to answer the questions or to raise the issue of racial discrimination against Japanese Americans. Chief Justice Stone signaled the end of the session, and the Court adjourned for the day.

PLeaDInG MInoru yasuI's case
Minoru Yasui's case came before the Court the following day. His attorney, Earl Bernard, began the arguments in *Yasui v. United States* by stating that Yasui had never renounced his citizenship, as Judge James Fee had claimed. The government lawyers had already acknowl-

edged that. Since he was a citizen, the lawyer argued, Yasui had been unjustly deprived of his rights by the lower court's ruling.

ACLU lawyer Wirin used the last half of the allotted time to denounce DeWitt's actions. Direct and focused, he aimed his ammunition at the military commander. The general, Wirin charged, had misused his power to discriminate against an entire racial group without cause or legal authority to do so. He accused DeWitt of acting on behalf of "pseudo-patriotic groups and the economic power groups wishing to acquire Japanese-owned lands at a song."

Using DeWitt's own racist words against him, Wirin claimed that the decision to evacuate Japanese Americans had nothing to do with national security. Neither Italian-American citizens nor those of German ancestry had been evacuated, even though Italy and Germany were also at war with the United States. "Race prejudice, not military necessity, was the reason for these orders," Wirin told the Court.

He debunked the claims in the Roberts report that Japanese Americans in Hawaii aided the enemy. Such claims, Wirin said, had been discounted by the Secretary of War and the U.S. Attorney General. Justice Roberts, who had overseen the Pearl Harbor commission that had issued the report, sat silently looking down from the bench.

In response to a question by Justice Black, Wirin outlined the situations when the Court should not pass judgment on military decisions. To escape judicial review, the military command must be responding to an emergency, must act in good faith, and must take steps to deal effectively with the situation. DeWitt's orders, Wirin said, did not meet any of those criteria. He noted that the military had six months in which to identify Japanese Americans guilty of aiding the enemy. Instead of taking this reasonable step to root out spies, the military condemned an entire race. His time up, Wirin returned to his seat at the defense table but not before commenting that "neither color nor race has any military significance."

In arguing the government's case, Solicitor General Fahy spent much of his time discussing the war powers of the president and Congress. Fahy was fifty-one years old in 1943 and had been a naval aviator during World War I. A graduate of Georgetown University Law School, he had been appointed solicitor general in 1941. In that post, he had appeared before the U.S. Supreme Court several times and kept a record of how many cases he won. With these cases, he aimed to add more victories to the tally.

Wartime gave extra weight to the government's power over citizens, Fahy argued. Under the Constitution, he said, the government had the power to override citizens' rights if necessary to protect the nation during war. Justice Jackson asked if war powers gave the government the right to discriminate against citizens of Japanese ancestry. "The circumstances of war," Fahy said, made the government's actions "reasonable." He denied that the evacuation and relocation of Japanese Americans were discriminatory.

Skillfully, Fahy steered the discussion to the war in the Pacific. He detailed the serious threat posed by the Japanese and the need to protect military bases on the West Coast from sabotage. Japanese Americans posed a threat, he claimed, because of their ties to the enemy nation. Some had been born in Japan, others had studied there. Even those who were American citizens had been raised in the Japanese culture. According to Fahy's argument, Japanese Americans "had never become assimilated" into American life. General DeWitt feared that they would betray the United States. His fear, the lawyer explained, was based on the population's ties to Japan and not on race. Fahy ignored the fact that many of the younger generation knew little of Japan, could not speak Japanese, and had been raised as Americans. He did not mention other Americans with cultural and ancestral ties to Germany, Italy, or other enemies of the United States.

Fahy ended his arguments with patriotic zeal, declaring that citizens had obligations as well as rights, particularly during war.

Since the *Korematsu* case dealt only with the question of whether Korematsu could appeal, lawyers and justices focused on legal terminology during oral arguments. There was no serious disagreement between the two sides over Korematsu's right to appeal. Justice Frankfurter curtly dismissed Wirin's view that his client had suffered harm even though the judge had not imposed a sentence. But no other justice offered objections. By the end of the discussion, it was obvious that the *Korematsu* lawyers would be arguing the case before the Court sometime in the near future.

"YOU MUST HAVE THE BODY"

While the justices deliberated on the *Yasui*, *Hirabayashi*, and *Korematsu* cases behind closed doors, the *Endo* appeal was making its way through the court system. After being fired from her job as a stenographer with the California State Highway Commission, Mitsuye Endo had been sent with other Japanese Americans to the Tule Lake War Relocation Center in Newell, California, in 1942. Her brother was serving in the U.S. army at the time.

With the help of lawyer James Purcell, Endo filed a

writ of habeas corpus in the U.S. District Court for the Northern District of California demanding to be set free. The petition was filed in July 1942.

Habeas corpus is a Latin term, literally meaning "you must have the body." A writ of habeas corpus demands that a prisoner be brought to court for a hearing to determine if officials followed legal procedures when detaining him or her. It provides a legal shield against the abuse of power by leaders who would imprison opponents illegally.

A person petitioning for such a writ must show that officials made an error in ordering the imprisonment. The writ of habeas corpus has been called "one of the

Mitsuye Endo types at her desk in the administrative office at the Topaz Relocation Center in Utah. She became the central figure in a 1944 Supreme Court case that challenged her imprisonment in the relocation center. The Court ruled in her favor, leading to the release of "loyal" U.S. citizens being held at the camps.

centerpieces of our liberties" as well as "the fundamental instrument for safeguarding individual freedom against arbitrary and lawless state action." The English Parliament adopted the Habeas Corpus Act in 1679 after the public demanded that lawmakers take action to prevent officials from illegally imprisoning citizens. America's founders incorporated the right into the U.S. Constitution's Article 1, which states: "The Privilege of the Writ of Habeas Corpus shall not be suspended, unless when in Cases of Rebellion or Invasion the public Safety may require it."

Under the writ of habeas corpus, people cannot be jailed "without due process of law" and without specified charges, the services of a lawyer, and a jury trial. These rights are guaranteed by the Fifth Amendment (in its due process clause) and the Sixth Amendment. The due process clause requires officials to follow legal procedures before depriving a citizen of life or liberty.

In Endo's petition for a writ of habeas corpus, Purcell contended that the U.S. government had no right to hold Endo, a loyal American citizen, born in the United States, who had no connection to Japan and was innocent of any wrongdoing. While her court case was pending, Endo applied for a permit to leave the prison camp.

The district court denied Purcell's petition in July 1943. The following month, the lawyer appealed the verdict to the Ninth Circuit Court of Appeals. Shortly afterward, Endo was transferred to the Topaz prison camp in central Utah.

In a bid to avoid a U.S. Supreme Court hearing on the case, government officials granted Endo's leave on August 16, 1943. The deal allowed Endo to leave the camp only if she agreed to drop her suit. In addition, officials barred her from returning to her home in

California. Instead of accepting the offer to leave, Endo chose to remain at the Topaz camp and pursue her bid for freedom through the courts. When the appeals court denied Endo's petition that August, it became clear that yet another case involving the exclusion, evacuation, and internment of Japanese Americans would be headed to the U.S. Supreme Court.

decisions rendered

On June 1, 1943, the U.S. Supreme Court ruled on Fred Korematsu's request for a hearing. Korematsu, the justices agreed, had a right to appeal his case even though the lower court judge had never imposed a sentence. In a unanimous decision, the Court sent the case back to the court of appeals for a ruling on Korematsu's claims that his evacuation from the West Coast violated his Constitutional rights.

Three weeks later, on June 21, the Court issued its ruling in the *Hirabayashi* case. Ignoring Hirabayashi's appeal of the evacuation conviction—the issue on which he had taken a stand—the Court ruled that he was guilty of a curfew violation. The military, Chief Justice Stone wrote in the unanimous decision, had the power to order a curfew as a "protective measure." Since the lower court had sentenced Hirabayashi to concurrent three-month jail sentences for both violations, Chief Justice Stone reasoned that if the Court upheld the curfew sentencing, it did not need to consider the evacuation charge.

In ruling against Hirabayashi, the Court stated that Congress, by passing Public Law 503, had ratified and approved the president's executive order. Congress had specifically mentioned a curfew during discussion of the bill, Stone noted. The military, thus authorized by the president and Congress, had the constitutional power to order the curfew:

> We conclude that it was within the constitutional power of Congress and the executive arm of the Government to prescribe this curfew order for the period under consideration and that its promulgation by the military commander involved no unlawful delegation of legislative power.

The Court relied on DeWitt's characterization of Japanese Americans to justify a curfew only for that racial group of citizens. Applying the curfew only to Japanese Americans, Stone wrote, was allowable because "in time of war residents having ethnic affiliations with an invading enemy may be a greater source of danger than those of a different ancestry."

In a concurring opinion, Justice Douglas acknowledged that the military, in fact, might have had time to review suspicious individuals rather than restrict an entire group. "But military decisions," he noted in justifying the Court's approval of the military action, "must be made without the benefit of hindsight."

Justice Murphy originally wrote a dissenting opinion, but under pressure changed it to concur with the majority view. As a recent appointee to the Court, he bowed to the views of his more experienced colleagues. In his concurrence, however, Murphy compared the treatment of Japanese Americans to that of Jews by the Germans. "Distinctions based on color and ancestry are utterly inconsistent with our traditions and ideals," Murphy stated in his separate opinion. "They are at variance with the principles for which we are now waging war."

Nevertheless, Murphy supported the decision because of "the critical military situation" after Pearl Harbor and the "urgent necessity of taking prompt and effective action" to protect against sabotage and espionage.

But Murphy also issued a caution:

> While this Court sits, it has the inescapable duty of seeing that the mandates of the Constitution are obeyed. That duty exists in time of war as well as in time of peace, and in its performance we must not forget that few indeed have been the invasions upon essential liberties which have not been accompanied by pleas of urgent necessity advanced in good faith by responsible men.

In his concurring opinion, Justice Rutledge said military officers should have "wide discretion" to oversee war operations. But he added the proviso that the Court could review military actions in cases where officers abused their power.

As a result of the decision, Hirabayashi went to Arizona, where he completed his sentence in a federal work camp. He had to arrange his own transportation, so he hitchhiked the 1,600 miles to the camp. A Quaker and a conscientious objector, he would later serve nine months at McNeil Island Federal Penitentiary after refusing to register for the draft.

That same day, the justices sent Yasui's case back to the lower courts. In their decision, they disagreed with Judge Fee's view that Yasui had forfeited his U.S. citizenship. But they upheld Yasui's conviction on violating the curfew, ruling that DeWitt's order could be applied to citizens. The Court based the decision on the previously issued *Hirabayashi* opinion. Because Yasui was a citizen, however, the justices recommended that the lower court reduce his prison sentence.

The Court decided both cases on the narrow issue of curfews. By doing so, the justices avoided making any judgment on the removal and forced detention of Japanese Americans. Civil rights activists now turned to the *Korematsu* and *Endo* cases for decisions on those issues.

MEMBERS OF THE U.S. SUPREME COURT WHO DECIDED THE *KOREMATSU* CASE. FRONT ROW, FROM LEFT: ASSOCIATE JUSTICES STANLEY F. REED AND OWEN J. ROBERTS, CHIEF JUSTICE HARLAN FISKE STONE, AND ASSOCIATE JUSTICES HUGO L. BLACK AND FELIX FRANKFURTER. BACK ROW, FROM LEFT: ASSOCIATE JUSTICES ROBERT H. JACKSON, WILLIAM O. DOUGLAS, FRANK MURPHY, AND WILEY B. RUTLEDGE.

FIVE
U.S. SUPREME COURT
ROUND II

AFTER THE U.S. SUPREME COURT RULING, Fred Korematsu's lawyers returned to court to appeal his conviction. Appearing before the Circuit Court of Appeals in San Francisco, they asked the judges to overturn the district court's ruling. As expected, the appeals court upheld Judge Adolphus St. Sure's decision against Korematsu.

While the court ruled on his fate, Korematsu spent his time digging ditches at the Topaz camp, where he lived with his family. The other Japanese Americans there had heard of Korematsu's case, and many shunned him because they believed his actions hurt their cause. Some thought the young man considered himself above them because he had refused to join the rest of the community at the camps, even after JACL leaders advised that course of action.

"It must have been very lonely for Fred. To make a personal stand like this, to stand apart from his community," commented a fellow detainee after the war. "Here he had not only been alienated from the larger society, the United States of America, but here he had disconnected himself from his community."

In September 1943 the War Department replaced General John DeWitt with General Delos C. Emmons.

LIFe aT TOPaZ ReLOCaTIOn center

When the Korematsu family stepped off the bus at Topaz Relocation Center, they entered a barren, desolate world of dust and discomfort. Built on flat lands in Utah's Sevier Desert, Topaz was in the west central section of the state, about 140 miles from Salt Lake City. Desert brush and bushes covered most of the surrounding land. Temperatures in summer soared to 115° F and dipped well below 0°F in winter. Housing provided little shelter.

Construction on the center began in July 1942. Several of the 623 buildings on the site had once served as camps for the Civilian Conservation Corps in the 1930s. The central section of Topaz consisted of thirty-four residential blocks, each divided into twelve barracks. Each barrack was further divided into six rooms, measuring about twenty feet by sixteen-to-twenty feet. Most of the eight thousand or so detainees who lived at the camp had lived in or near San Francisco.

The Korematsu family, like others at the center, occupied a single room. In some cases, two families had to share a room. Seventy or more families housed in each residential block shared a dining hall, a recreation area, and a community bathroom/laundry facility.

The family's new home was in a tarpaper barracks, separated from neighbors by thin, pine boards that did not reach the roof. A potbellied stove provided heat. The only other furniture was an army cot with one blanket for each person. A lightbulb hung from the ceiling. Running water was available only at the communal washrooms.

The day began with a blast from a siren at 7 a.m. People stood in line for meals, to go to the bathroom, and to use the laundry. Food was rationed, as it was in outside communities. But unlike those outside, the detainees had no choice over the menu. They dined most often on hot-dogs, macaroni, rice, dried fish, and pickled vegetables.

Additional food included beef from the camp's cattle ranch and hogs, chickens, turkeys, and vegetables raised at the complex. Detainees worked in the fields, mined coal in the area, and filled most of the menial jobs at the camp. Workers received low wages that often did not cover the costs for clothing and other essentials.

While the adults worked, the children attended school in the barracks. At first, students had to sit on the floor with no books and no school supplies. Eventually, the makeshift schools were equipped with chairs, desks, and donated textbooks. Because few teachers wanted to move to the camps, college-educated evacuees often filled in as instructors. Like their contemporaries in schools throughout the nation, students began their day with the Pledge of Allegiance, "with liberty and justice for all."

As time went on, Japanese Americans transformed their surroundings as best they could. They planted flowers, built furniture from wood scrounged from the scrap heap, dug wading pools, and sewed clothing. Men built partitions in the one-room units, put up shelves, and painted with supplies bought from a catalog. Women fashioned beautiful designs from seashells found on the grounds where an ancient lake had once been. Children attended dance and music classes, and two orchestras performed for their fellow residents.

Community councils made up of detainees served as a liaison between residents and camp administrators. WRA officials, however, had the final say over camp policy and operations. The camp published its own newspaper, edited and written by residents but overseen by a WRA officer. A hospital at the camp provided health care, although the facility ran short of supplies and had too few medical staff members to serve the population.

Boy Scouts and Girl Scouts operated local chapters at the camp, and residents could join the YMCA, YWCA, and the American Red Cross. Churches held services on site, all but the banned Shinto religion because of its worship of Japan's emperor.

Even with the clubs, schools, and other activities, daily life at the camps was far from normal. A barbed-wire fence ran around the entire perimeter of the camp. A sentry post guarded the entrance and armed guards in seven watchtowers kept an eye on all that happened in and around the camp. On April 11, 1943, guards shot and killed a sixty-three-year-old detainee, James Hatsuaki Wakasa, who wandered too close to the fence. As a result of that incident, the WRA moved the guards farther from the residences and restricted their use of guns.

Nevertheless, the presence of armed guards and barbed wire instilled fear. They reinforced the fact that the Japanese Americans inside the camps were prisoners. One man who spent part of his childhood in a camp recalled life there:

"I remember the barbed wire fence from which my parents warned me to stay away. I remember the sight of high guard towers. I remember soldiers carrying rifles, and I remember being afraid."

Emmons had overseen military operations in Hawaii and had resisted pressure to evacuate Japanese Americans from the islands. The new commander began working on a plan to free most of the detainees and allow them to return to the West Coast. President Franklin Roosevelt did not support the plan, however. He favored a much more gradual resettlement of Japanese Americans. In June 1944, Roosevelt reassigned Emmons to another post.

Even though he no longer served as commander of the West Coast, DeWitt continued to wield influence. The War Department released DeWitt's *Final Report* in January 1944. As expected, it reiterated the unsubstantiated rumors and charges against Japanese-American saboteurs. DeWitt relied on racial traits, lumping together all ethnic Japanese to make his case for wholesale removal of Japanese Americans from the West Coast.

On February 2, 1944, Korematsu's lawyers petitioned the U.S. Supreme Court for a hearing. They filed the brief for Korematsu on February 8, 1944. In the brief, they argued that the exclusion order issued by General DeWitt violated the Fourth, Fifth, Sixth, Eighth, and Thirteenth amendments of the Constitution. In addition, they said, the statute unlawfully gave the military unlimited power to decide the fate of Japanese Americans. The courts, not the military, should be the ones to judge guilt or innocence of civilians. The case, the brief concluded, presented issues of "great gravity" that would affect not only Japanese Americans but also "the rights and liberties" of all U.S. citizens. The Constitution itself was on trial, according to the brief. "Whether this nation may, with truth, be identified as a republican democracy or whether, because of public apathy and indifference, it has surrendered all governmental power to the executive division without a struggle are the fundamental questions this Court must decide."

Solicitor General Charles Fahy, again representing the U.S. government in the case, argued in his brief that the Court should deny Korematsu's request for a hearing. The previously decided *Hirabayashi* ruling, he said, had already settled the matters to be raised. Even though Korematsu's removal to a guarded prison camp resulted in far greater losses than the annoyance of a curfew, Fahy concluded, the *Hirabayashi* ruling should still apply.

The American Civil Liberties Union also filed a brief in support of Korematsu's request for a hearing.

In March, the man at the center of the case, Fred Korematsu, was approved for an "indefinite leave" from the Topaz camp to work at a machine shop in Detroit. Because of his conviction, he had to report to a probation officer every month.

presenting the government's case

On March 27, 1944, the Supreme Court agreed to hear Korematsu's case. Both sides would have about a month to file briefs in the case. The Court scheduled oral arguments for May 1, 1944. The Roosevelt administration did not want the Court to decide the case before the upcoming elections in November. In an effort to delay the decision, government lawyers argued that they needed more time to prepare the case. The Court responded by setting oral arguments for October 11 and 12, 1944. Mitsuye Endo's case would be argued at the same time.

Three groups submitted *amicus curiae* briefs in the *Korematsu* case. The ACLU and the Japanese American Citizens League backed Korematsu. The states of California, Oregon, and Washington again filed a brief that reflected the War Department's position.

In his brief to the Court, Fahy called on the Court to

uphold Korematsu's conviction. He presented four points to justify the exclusion order:

1. The president's order, Executive Order No. 9066, gave the military the authority to establish military zones in the West Coast and to exclude "any or all persons" from those areas. In passing Public Law 503, Congress, too, consented to military control over such matters.

2. The order was not unconstitutional; it was "a valid exercise of the war power." The need for national security called for the military to evacuate Japanese Americans. The Constitution allowed such action, even though it restricted citizens' liberty because it was a "military necessity."

3. The Court should consider only the question of Korematsu's conviction of resisting a military order. It should not examine the broader issue of the detention of Japanese Americans in camps.

4. Even if the Court were to rule on the detention, such action was allowed under the war powers granted the Congress and the president.

As in the *Hirabayashi* case, the solicitor general did not include any reference to the Ringle report or suggestions that General DeWitt's claims might be false.

The brief submitted for the states of California, Washington, and Oregon again relied on General DeWitt's arguments for excluding Japanese Americans from the West Coast. Echoing the general's previous claims, the lawyers argued that the entire population of Japanese Americans had to be removed to protect national security. The military lacked time and technical ability to determine the loyalty of more than 100,000 Japanese Americans in the area, the brief contended. Therefore, the lawyers argued, "it was reasonable for the military commander to meet the danger threatened from the unidentified disloyal members of the group by excluding the group as a whole." The lawyers used results from the Loyalty Questionnaire to show that some Japanese Americans were disloyal. In a footnote, they quoted a commentary that DeWitt "doubtless acted on such intelligence as was available."

on korematsu's side

The California ACLU, headed by Ernest Besig, and Wayne Collins, the San Francisco lawyer representing Korematsu, had serious disagreements with the national ACLU legal team about how to handle the case. National ACLU officials threatened to cut off funding for the appeal. Collins and the California ACLU, however, stood their ground and developed the case for Korematsu. "We didn't give in to the national office and said, 'Look, go ahead. We believe we took the right position and we're going to stand by Fred,'" Besig recalled years later.

As in the *Hirabayashi* case, the major disagreement focused on the extent of the president's war powers. Nevertheless, the two briefs argued many of the same points. In his ninety-eight-page brief, Collins focused on four arguments:

1. The president's order did not give the military authority to evacuate Japanese Americans and send them to guarded prison camps.
2. Congress did not authorize or approve such a plan.
3. The law and the orders establishing such a plan violated Korematsu's constitutional rights.

4. Racial prejudice, not any threat to national security, led the military to order the exclusion, evacuation, and detention of Japanese Americans.

The *amicus* brief filed by the American Civil Liberties Union argued that Korematsu's case involved more than his exclusion from a section of the West Coast. "The true issue posed by this case," the brief stated, "is whether or not a citizen of the United States may, because he is of Japanese ancestry, be confined in barbed wire stockades euphemistically termed Assembly Centers or Relocation Centers—actually concentration camps."

General DeWitt's orders, the brief noted, not only required Japanese Americans to vacate the area but also demanded that they turn themselves in to be shipped to guarded prison camps. The brief urged the Court to condemn such imprisonment of American citizens, "without charges, without trial, without conviction, without any safeguards whatever."

"If this can be permitted under the Constitution," the brief argued, "much of Germany's anti-Semitic program can be duplicated in this country with no violation of constitutional rights."

The lengthiest brief, filed by the JACL, once again argued that there was "no reasonable basis for the military exclusion" of West Coast Japanese Americans. Because no military necessity existed, the brief contended, the exclusion was unconstitutional. Saburo Kido of the JACL and A. L. Wirin, who served as counsel to both the JACL and the ACLU, wrote the two-hundred-page document. The lawyers refuted, point by point, DeWitt's claims that Japanese Americans posed a threat to the nation. A long list of newspaper articles and sociological studies backed their arguments. They did not have access, as Fahy did, to the Ringle report or the FBI and FCC information that proved DeWitt wrong.

Before the court

On October 11, 1944, the attorneys gathered at the Supreme Court for oral arguments in the *Korematsu* and *Endo* cases. James Purcell took his place as the attorney representing Mitsuye Endo. Korematsu's lawyer, Wayne Collins, would split his time before the Court with ACLU attorney Charles Horsky. As a concession to the national ACLU, the Northern California ACLU had agreed to let Horsky assist Collins in his defense of Korematsu. Solicitor General Fahy would present arguments for the government in both cases. The same nine justices took their places in front of the velvet curtain.

For five hours the justices and attorneys in the two cases held a vigorous discussion on the issues involved. No transcript or recording of the session exists. According to writer and researcher Peter Irons, who wrote about the case in the 1983 book *Justice at War*, Collins began arguments with an attack on the military necessity of DeWitt's exclusion order. Irons based his report on a Court observer's notes of the oral arguments. Korematsu could not be charged under an order that was not justified, Collins presumably argued.

Horsky reportedly focused his arguments on building a connection between the charge against Korematsu and detention. If Korematsu had obeyed the evacuation order, according to the argument, he would have been forced to go to an assembly center, where he would have been detained. According to Irons, Horsky argued that such a detention of a citizen was illegal. Therefore, Korematsu could not be punished for trying to avoid being unlawfully detained.

Taking his turn before the bench, Fahy argued that the detention of Japanese Americans should not be considered in the *Korematsu* case. Korematsu had been charged with being in a forbidden area in violation of the evacuation order. According to Irons, the solicitor general insisted that the case involved only evacuation, which was justified because of national security.

The following day, attorney Purcell made the case for Endo. Irons reported that the lawyer carefully detailed the history of the case for the Court. He followed with an attack on the government's detention of loyal citizens. Congress, he argued, had never authorized the military to hold loyal American citizens under armed guard.

In what Irons called a "half-hearted" defense, Fahy argued that Japanese Americans had been detained for "preventive" reasons. The government would not allow Endo to return to the West Coast for her own good. Residents there presumably would be hostile to Endo, "and there would be repercussions." The military had the power to order the evacuation, Fahy argued; therefore, it had the power to enforce the detention because the evacuation required it.

Chief Justice Harlan Stone replied: "The war power is a power for the prosecution of war . . . not a power to repair injuries which the war has produced."

SIX
THE DECISION

On December 17, 1944, the U.S. Army announced that as of January 2, 1945, Japanese Americans would no longer be excluded from the West Coast. Commenting on the army's report, Defense Secretary Harold Ickes said he did not expect to see a "hasty mass movement" of Japanese Americans back to the area.

Only twenty-four hours later, on December 18, 1944, reporters gathered at the U.S. Supreme Court to hear the justices' decisions on the internment cases. Justice Hugo Black, author of the majority decision, read the Court's ruling on the *Korematsu* case.

In a six to three decision, the justices upheld Fred Korematsu's conviction. According to the Court, the Constitution allowed the military to exclude Japanese Americans from the West Coast. In making their decision, the justices relied on the *Hirabayashi* case, even while acknowledging that removal from one's home far outweighed the hardship of a curfew. Korematsu was guilty, they said, of violating a military order to leave. In its ruling, the Court considered only Korematsu's exclusion from the West Coast. The decision did not address the imprisonment in armed camps of Korematsu and other Japanese Americans.

Surprisingly, Justice Black and Justice William

Douglas—both well-known human rights advocates—voted with the majority. Black noted, in the decision, that laws that restrict the civil rights of one racial group were "immediately suspect." He went on to say, however, that such laws were not necessarily unconstitutional. "Pressing public necessity" might justify the laws, he wrote, although "racial antagonism" could not.

As they had in the *Hirabayashi* case, the justices ruled that the military, as authorized under Congress, had the power "to say who should, and who should not, remain in the threatened areas." Once again, the Court relied on General John DeWitt's word that Japanese Americans threatened the nation's security. Based on that, the Court ruled that the government had the power to exclude ethnic Japanese to prevent threats to the nation. Noting the great deprivation caused by the exclusion order, Black said the Constitution would allow such a measure only in cases identified by authorized military officials as of "the gravest imminent danger to the public safety."

The Court upheld Korematsu's conviction, the justice wrote, "because we could not reject the finding of the military authorities that it was impossible to bring about an immediate segregation of the disloyal from the loyal." Black disputed the petitioner's description of the camps, which he said could not fairly be called concentration camps "with all the ugly connotations that term implies."

In justifying the decision, Black pointed to the Japanese Americans who had refused to swear loyalty on the forms administered at the camps. "That there were members of the group who retained loyalties to Japan has been confirmed by investigations made subsequent to the exclusion," Black wrote.

Black rejected Korematsu's contention that his exclusion and later imprisonment in a concentration camp was racially motivated. Korematsu was not excluded because of his race, according to Black, but because of military necessity. "There was evidence of disloyalty on the part of some, the military authorities considered that the need for action was great, and time was short," he noted. He added that Congress had determined that military leaders should have the power to act as they had.

Justice Felix Frankfurter, in a separate concurring opinion, added a strong defense of the war powers granted under the Constitution. He noted that the Constitution granted Congress and the president "the power to wage war successfully." And while noting that the Constitution limits war powers, Frankfurter said that military actions must be judged "wholly in the context of war." He saw nothing in DeWitt's order to make it invalid.

"INTO THE UGLY ABYSS OF RACISM"

The justices in the minority denounced the exclusion and forced detention of citizens. In three separate dissents, Justices Owen Roberts, Frank Murphy, and Robert Jackson charged that DeWitt's orders violated Constitutional rights and illegally targeted one race.

Roberts, who had investigated the matter for the administration, called the exclusion "a clear violation of Constitutional rights." The justice said he could support the curfew order as a "mild and temporary deprivation of liberty." The exclusion, on the other hand, had far more serious consequences. "It is the case," he said, "of convicting a citizen as a punishment for not submitting to imprisonment in a concentration camp, based on his ancestry, and solely because of his ancestry, without evidence or inquiry concerning his loyalty and good disposition towards the United States." Unlike Black, Roberts had no hesitation in labeling the relocation centers as concentration camps.

The exclusion should be judged as "part of an over-all plan for forceable detention," Roberts said. Ruling on just the narrow issue of exclusion, he added, "is to shut our eyes to reality." DeWitt's two orders—one to leave the area and the other to stay put—left Korematsu with little choice, Roberts said. The orders, he added, were "nothing but a cleverly devised trap to accomplish the real purpose of the military authority, which was to lock him up in a concentration camp."

Murphy used even harsher language to attack the decision in his dissent. The exclusion, he said, "goes over 'the very brink of constitutional power' and falls into the ugly abyss of racism." He agreed with other justices that the judgment of military leaders must be treated with great respect. However, military power—like that of any other branch of government—must not be exempt from review by the courts.

The order banishing Japanese Americans from the West Coast was "one of the most sweeping and complete deprivations of constitutional rights in the history of this nation in the absence of martial law," Murphy charged. DeWitt did not base his orders on valid evidence, the justice said, but rather on racial stereotypes derived from "misinformation, half-truths and insinuations."

Murphy acknowledged that some Japanese Americans might have tried to aid the enemy. But the American system of law requires that people are punished only for their own actions, not those of others. He noted that the Court's approval of such military orders supported "the abhorrent and despicable treatment of minority groups by the dictatorial tyrannies which this nation is now pledged to destroy."

Concluding his stinging dissent, Murphy called the majority opinion a "legalization of racism." He noted that all Americans had ties to foreign nations and that all resi-

Associate Justice Frank Murphy, who charged in his dissenting opinion in *Korematsu* v. *United States* that the Court's sanction of the wartime internment of Japanese Americans amounted to a "legalization of racism."

dents should be treated "as the heirs of the American experiment." He ended with a sharp rebuke:

> Racial discrimination in any form and in any degree has no justifiable part whatever in our democratic way of life. It is unattractive in any setting but it is utterly revolting among a free people who have embraced the principles set forth in the Constitution of the United States.

In his dissent, Jackson, too, attacked DeWitt's orders as racially based. Korematsu's only crime, he noted, was merely "being present" in his home state of California. The charges against him arose "not from anything he did, said, or thought . . . but only in that he was born of different racial stock."

During war, the military's primary goal is for its measures to be successful, rather than legal, according to Jackson. But the courts must fulfill their role as well: to protect individual rights when military might threatens liberty. In setting the correct balance between military necessity and individual rights, the court must judge whether military actions are necessary. The Court, Jackson noted, faced hurdles when trying to determine whether DeWitt's orders were necessary:

> How does the Court know that these orders have a reasonable basis in necessity? No evidence whatever on that subject has been taken by this or any other court. There is sharp controversy as to the credibility of the DeWitt report. So the Court, having no real evidence before it, has no choice but to accept General DeWitt's own unsworn, self-serving statement, untested by any cross-examination, that what he did was reasonable.

But even when a military order "is a reasonable exercise of military authority," Jackson said, the courts cannot enforce it if it violates rights guaranteed under the Constitution. "The courts can exercise only the judicial power, can apply only law, and must abide by the Constitution," he concluded, "or they cease to be civil courts and become instruments of military policy."

The majority ruling, Jackson said, posed even more danger to democracy than DeWitt's order because it endorsed racial discrimination and the violation of citizens' rights. Such a precedent, he charged, "lies about like a loaded weapon" that future authorities can use to take control.

John Frank, who served as clerk to Justice Black, later suggested that the justices in the majority believed they had a duty, as patriotic Americans, to back the president and the military, even if it meant ignoring the Constitution. Black, whom Frank described as "an intensely patriotic man," took the word of DeWitt that the action was a matter of national defense. "In wartime," noted the former clerk, "he was not going to quarrel with a general about what a general thought was a military necessity."

Patriotism, however, did not exempt the justices from their duty as guardians of the Constitution, said researcher Peter Irons. They should have asked for proof, he said, to back up DeWitt's claims. "Every branch of the government that is responsible for protecting the Constitution failed . . . . the Supreme Court literally abandoned its role of asking probing questions."

The decision stunned civil libertarians throughout the country. Ernest Besig of the Northern California ACLU said that of the eight cases his organization argued before the U.S. Supreme Court, the only one it lost was the *Korematsu* suit. "The shocking thing is that we lost the case of racial discrimination against Japanese," he said years later.

An editorial in *The New York Times* said the Court may have ruled that the removal of Japanese Americans was constitutional, but "whether it was right and necessary . . . is another story." The writer noted that ethnic Japanese allowed to remain in Hawaii had done no harm. The editorial urged communities to accept returning Japanese Americans cheerfully "for the sake of America's reputation for fair play."

For Korematsu, the decision came as a blow, but he resolved not to despair. "I was dumbfounded," he admitted. "But I continued on. I said I'm an American and just as long as I'm in this country . . . I will keep on going and if there is a chance of reopening the case, I will do it."

That chance came, but not for thirty-nine years.

RULInG In THe *ENDO* case

On the same day the Court issued the *Korematsu* decision, it ruled on the *Endo* case. In a decision written by Justice Douglas, the Court ordered the WRA to release Mitsuye Endo. The camps had no authority to hold loyal citizens, according to the opinion. The justices, however, once again refused to address whether the president and Congress had the constitutional authority to set up the camp system aimed at Japanese Americans. The decision applied only to citizens proven to be loyal:

> [W]hatever power the War Relocation Authority may have to detain other classes of citizens, it has no authority to subject citizens who are concededly loyal to its leave procedure.

Congress and the president authorized the military to take action, Douglas concluded, but only for the "precise purpose" of protecting "against espionage and sabotage." A citizen who had been proven loyal "presents no problem of espionage or sabotage," he noted. Neither the executive order nor Congress's law had ever intended that loyal citizens should be held against their will, according to Douglas. Ignoring the racial overtones of DeWitt's statements and actions, Douglas noted that loyalty was "a matter of the heart and mind not of race, creed, or color." He reiterated the contention that the evacuation was necessary as a war measure, not as an action against a particular race.

Justices Murphy and Roberts, both of whom had dissented in the *Korematsu* case, filed separate concurring opinions in *Endo*. As he had in the previous case, Murphy blasted the detention of Japanese Americans as "not only unauthorized by Congress or the Executive but [as] another example of the unconstitutional resort to racism inherent in the entire evacuation program."

Roberts aimed his attack at the president and Congress as well. The Court should have ruled on the "serious constitutional question" raised by their conduct, he said. Roberts argued that both branches of government knew exactly what DeWitt planned regarding the evacuation and forced detention of Japanese Americans. According to Roberts, the Roosevelt administration issued regulations and a handbook on the military operation. Congress reviewed the "full details" of the plans for evacuation and detention before approving funding for the WRA.

The actions approved by Congress and the president "violated the guarantees of the Bill of Rights . . . especially the guarantee of due process of law," according to Roberts. To lay the blame on underlings who exceeded their authority—and not on the president and Congress—"is to hide one's head in the sand," he wrote. It was the Court's responsibility, he said, to protect those rights by ruling on the constitutional issues involved.

DETENTION ENDED

The *Endo* ruling and the U.S. Army's decision to lift the exclusion opened the way to the release of the 61,000 Japanese Americans still in the camps, with the exception of those at Tule Lake. About 18,700 detainees who had been judged disloyal continued to be held at Tule Lake. The government finally closed that camp in 1946.

The WRA gave each person $25 or each family $50 and train fare home. Once at their destination, however, many found they had no home. Property had been stolen, businesses closed, and homes and farms taken over by others. In 1948, Congress approved payments of more than $37 million to settle 26,578 claims from Japanese Americans detained during the war.

A year after the *Korematsu* decision, the U.S. Supreme Court ruled, in *Duncan* v. *Kahanamoku*, that civilians had been unconstitutionally tried under martial law in Hawaii. The justices again cited the *Milligan* case, but this time they used the previous ruling to overturn the charges against a Japanese American. Over the next decade, the Court ruled against racial discrimination, strengthened citizens' rights to due process, and took a number of other stands that contradicted the actions allowed in the *Korematsu* decision. However, the Court has never directly overturned the *Korematsu* ruling.

Two later Court rulings established that presidents do not have inherent powers, even in wartime. In 1952, the Court disallowed President Harry S. Truman's seizure of steel mills to prevent a strike during the Korean War. Truman claimed the strike threatened national defense. This time, however, Congress did not back the president's action. Truman said he had the authority to seize the steel mills under the war powers granted him as president, the same claim used by the government in *Korematsu*. In ruling against the action, the U.S. Supreme Court said that war powers did not give the president the right to override the Constitution.

Again in 1971 the Court ruled against a president, this time Richard Nixon, when he used national defense as grounds to stop the printing of the Pentagon Papers. The papers were a massive, classified report on America's disastrous handling of the Vietnam War, from 1945 to 1968. Nixon argued that information in the documents would jeopardize the nation's current war efforts and that as commander in chief, he had the power to prevent *The New York Times* and the *Washington Post* from publishing them. The Court disagreed. In a six to three decision, the Court ruled that the Nixon administration had failed to prove its case. Justice Hugo L. Black, in his concurring opinion, noted that if the Court allowed the president the "inherent power" to stop the presses to protect the nation, it "would wipe out the First Amendment and destroy the fundamental liberty and security of the very people the Government hopes to make 'secure.'"

A private citizen

After Fred Korematsu lost his case, he quietly returned to being a private citizen. Because of his conviction, he had a criminal record, which made it difficult at times to get work. After spending two years at the Topaz camp, he moved to Salt Lake City and later Detroit. Eventually, he settled in California, where he worked as a draftsman. He chose not to discuss the case. Not even his daughter knew of his role in the landmark decision until a discussion during her high school social studies class touched on the case.

During the 1960s and 1970s, African Americans led by the Rev. Martin Luther King Jr. pushed for equality and an end to discrimination based on race. The successes inspired a similar call for equal treatment of Japanese Americans. At the urging of Japanese-American leaders and other civil rights activists, President Jimmy Carter established the Commission on Wartime Relocation and Internment of Civilians in 1980. The commission reviewed the treatment of Japanese Americans during World War II. In its final report, issued in 1983, the commission concluded that racism and not national security had prompted the exclusion and internment of the West Coast Japanese Americans.

In 1983, Irons, a lawyer who was researching the Japanese internment for a book, discovered government documents that shed new light on the case. The documents proved that the government lawyers who argued the case

PRESIDENT JIMMY CARTER SIGNS A BILL CREATING THE COMMISSION ON WARTIME RELOCATION AND INTERNMENT OF CIVILIANS ON JULY 31, 1980. THE COMMISSION EXAMINED THE TREATMENT OF JAPANESE AMERICANS DURING WORLD WAR II AND CONCLUDED THAT RACISM, NOT NATIONAL SECURITY CONCERNS, LED TO THEIR INTERNMENT. WITNESSING THE SIGNING ARE, FROM LEFT, SENATOR DANIEL INOUYE, D-HAWAII, WHO LOST AN ARM AS A MEMBER OF THE FAMED 442ND REGIMENTAL COMBAT TEAM; REPRESENTATIVE NORMAN MINETA, D-CALIFORNIA, WHO WAS INTERNED WITH HIS FAMILY AT HEART MOUNTAIN CAMP IN WYOMING; SENATOR SPARK MATSUNAGA, D-HAWAII, WHO RECEIVED TWO PURPLE HEARTS FOR HIS MILITARY SERVICE WITH THE 100TH INFANTRY BATTALION; AND REPRESENTATIVE GEORGE DANIELSON, D-CALIFORNIA, WHO COSPONSORED THE BILL.

before the Supreme Court knew General DeWitt's claims of sabotage by Japanese Americans were false. According to Irons, the FBI, the FCC, and naval intelligence officers all discounted the general's views. None of the three agencies could find a single case of sabotage among Japanese Americans. This information was contained in a report compiled by Lt. Commander Kenneth Ringle and given to DeWitt. The government's case rested on DeWitt's *Final Report* in which the general used bogus reports of sabotage to justify the evacuation of Japanese Americans. During his research, Irons uncovered notes from Justice Department lawyer Edward Ennis to Solicitor General Charles Fahy, urging the legal team to tell the Court the truth. But Fahy, who headed the government's legal team, vetoed the idea. As a result, the U.S. Supreme Court never saw the documents that discounted DeWitt's claims.

seven
JUSTICE AT LAST

Peter Irons knew the documents he had found could have a dramatic impact on the *Korematsu* case and the others filed by Japanese Americans during World War II. At long last, they might force the courts to rule on whether the internment was unconstitutional. Any attempt to reopen the cases, however, would put the spotlight on Fred Korematsu. It would also intensify the furor over the treatment of Japanese Americans ignited by the Commission on Wartime Relocation and Internment's report.

Irons took his findings to Korematsu, then in his sixties. After he looked at the papers, Korematsu agreed to take the case back to court. There was "no question in my mind," he said about the decision to reopen a case he had not talked about for forty years. "I was prepared to do it and I wanted to do it." Lawyers at the Asian Law Caucus volunteered to represent Korematsu in the case.

The legal team, led by Dale Minami and other young lawyers from the Caucus, decided against filing their claim with the U.S. Supreme Court. Such an action had never been tried before, and they feared the case would be thrown out on procedural grounds. Instead they pursued the case in federal court, at the U.S. District Court in San Francisco.

The three Japanese-American men whose landmark Supreme Court cases challenged U.S. internment and exclusion policies during World War II speak at a press conference on January 19, 1983. Federal courts later overturned the men's convictions. From left, Fred Korematsu, Minoru Yasui, and Gordon Hirabayashi.

Korematsu's lawyers used a legal maneuver so rare that even the judge had never dealt with it in court before. They filed a *writ of coram nobis* in U.S. District Court on Korematsu's behalf. The term *coram nobis* is Latin, meaning "before us." By filing the writ, Korematsu's lawyers claimed that an error had been committed in court and that it needed to be corrected. They based their claims on the newly discovered documents that revealed the government lawyers' deception.

During a break in the hearing on the case, the government offered to pardon Korematsu if he dropped the suit. Korematsu's attorneys told him of the proposal. "It's Fred's position that the government should seek a pardon from him," Korematsu's wife, Kathryn, replied. The hearing resumed.

On November 10, 1983, nearly forty years after the U.S. Supreme Court had issued its original ruling, Korematsu finally got his chance to speak out against the internment and the decision that sanctioned it. As the sixty-four-year-old Korematsu rose to sit in the witness chair, every eye in the packed courtroom followed him.

"Forty years ago I came into this courtroom in handcuffs and I was sent to a camp," he told federal judge Marilyn Hall Patel. "The camp was not fit for human habitation. Horse stalls are for horses, not for people." The courtroom remained silent as Korematsu urged the judge to reverse his conviction not only for himself but for the entire nation. The discrimination that led to his conviction, he noted, could be leveled against any citizen who looked different or came from a different culture.

The judge agreed. Without waiting to write a formal opinion, she ruled from the bench that same day. In granting Korematsu his motion to clear his name, Judge Patel delivered a stinging rebuke to the government. The new evidence, she said, showed that the government had suppressed evidence and was guilty of misconduct during the original trials. In addition, she said, the government policies that led to the evacuation and forced detention of Japanese Americans were tainted with racism. The claim that the evacuation and detention had to be carried out because of military necessity, the judge ruled, was based on "unsubstantiated facts, distortions and representations of at least one military commander [John DeWitt], whose views were seriously infected by racism."

In her written opinion on the case issued five months later, Judge Patel noted that the records showed the government had "deliberately omitted relevant information and provided misleading information and papers before the Court." When law enforcement officers "violate their ethical obligations to the Court" in such a manner, she wrote, "the judicial process is seriously impaired."

Judge Patel took the government to task for its deplorable behavior in the *Korematsu* case. The decision, which the U.S. Supreme Court has yet to overturn, "stands as a constant caution that in times of war or declared military necessity our institutions must be vigilant in protecting constitutional guarantees," Judge Patel said. She added:

> [I]n times of distress the shield of military necessity and national security must not be used to protect governmental actions from close scrutiny and accountability. . . . [I]n times of international hostility and antagonisms our institutions, legislative, executive and judicial, must be prepared to exercise their authority to protect all citizens from the petty fears and prejudices that are so easily aroused.

As the significance of the ruling began to sink in, members of the audience—many of whom had been interned in the World War II camps—began to cry. "The crowd came up to me, and they put their arms around me and hugged me," Fred Korematsu recalled. "A lot of them were in tears." For Korematsu, the long battle to clear his name was over. But his involvement in the fight to preserve civil rights for all would continue.

Two other key players in the Japanese-American cases shared Fred Korematsu's victory in court. Gordon Hirabayashi won his petition for *coram nobis* in U.S.

MATORU ETO, 107 YEARS OLD, RECEIVES A CHECK AND A LETTER OF APOLOGY
FROM PRESIDENT GEORGE H. W. BUSH ON OCTOBER 9, 1990, DURING A SPE-
CIAL CEREMONY IN THE GREAT HALL OF THE U.S. DEPARTMENT OF JUSTICE
IN WASHINGTON, D.C. ETO WAS ONE OF THE OLDEST LIVING JAPANESE
AMERICANS TO BE INTERNED DURING WORLD WAR II. CONGRESS APPROVED
REPARATION CHECKS FOR ALL LIVING VICTIMS OF THE ENFORCED RELOCATION.

THE WHITE HOUSE

WASHINGTON

A monetary sum and words alone cannot restore lost years or erase painful memories; neither can they fully convey our Nation's resolve to rectify injustice and to uphold the rights of individuals. We can never fully right the wrongs of the past. But we can take a clear stand for justice and recognize that serious injustices were done to Japanese Americans during World War II.

In enacting a law calling for restitution and offering a sincere apology, your fellow Americans have, in a very real sense, renewed their traditional commitment to the ideals of freedom, equality, and justice. You and your family have our best wishes for the future.

Sincerely,

[signature: G. Bush]

AFTER CONGRESS APPROVED THE CIVIL LIBERTIES ACT OF 1988, THE U.S. GOVERNMENT ISSUED CHECKS TO JAPANESE AMERICANS HELD IN CAMPS DURING WORLD WAR II, AND PRESIDENT GEORGE H. W. BUSH ISSUED THIS LETTER OF APOLOGY.

District Court in Seattle, Washington, more than forty years after the U.S. Supreme Court found him guilty of a curfew violation. The court in 1986 also overturned his conviction for resisting the exclusion order. "It was a vindication of all the effort people had put in for the rights of citizens during crisis periods," he said in an interview in 2000. "The U.S. government admitted it made a mistake. A country that can do that is a strong country. I have more faith and allegiance to the Constitution than I ever had before."

In 1984, the U.S. District Court in Portland, Oregon, overturned Minoru Yasui's conviction of a curfew viola-tion. However, Judge Robert C. Belloni rejected Yasui's bid that the court find the government guilty of miscon-duct and DeWitt's proclamation unconstitutional. Yasui appealed, but the U.S. Supreme Court dismissed the case after Yasui died in 1986.

The court victories, however, provided the push needed for Congress finally to address the "grave in justice" done to Japanese Americans during World War II. The 1988 Civil Liberties Act, passed in August of that year, issued an apology and authorized payments of $20,000 to each of those held in the camps. President George H. W. Bush signed the letter of apology that accompanied the checks sent to former internees on November 21, 1989. The act also provided for review of convictions arising from the evacuation and detention. The so-called redress movement focused attention on the treatment of Japanese Americans during the war.

In January 1998, President Bill Clinton presented Fred Korematsu with the Medal of Freedom, the nation's highest civilian award. "In the long history of our

PRESIDENT BILL CLINTON CONGRATULATES FRED KOREMATSU AFTER AWARDING HIM THE PRESIDENTIAL MEDAL OF FREEDOM, THE NATION'S HIGHEST CIVILIAN HONOR, DURING CEREMONIES AT THE WHITE HOUSE ON JANUARY 15, 1998. KOREMATSU LOST HIS LANDMARK SUPREME COURT CASE PROTESTING THE EXCLUSION OF JAPANESE AMERICANS FROM THE WEST COAST DURING WORLD WAR II, BUT HIS EFFORTS LATER LED TO REPARATIONS FOR U.S. MISTREATMENT OF JAPANESE AMERICANS DURING THE WAR.

country's constant search for justice, some names of ordinary citizens stand for millions of souls, Plessy, Brown, Parks," said Clinton as he listed the names of American heroes in the fight for civil rights. "To that distinguished list, today we add the name of Fred Korematsu."

U.S. Representative Ellen Tauscher, D-California, witnessed the presentation and added her words of praise for Korematsu. "Every American owes Mr. Korematsu a debt of gratitude for having the courage, in an era of great hostility, to stand up for his constitutional rights," she said.

Proud and touched by the gesture, Korematsu said he hoped his story would remind others that discrimination can be aimed at anyone. "It will give recognition that if they ever do try to start anything like that again—they will have to think twice before they do it," he said.

Those prophetic words would gain new meaning for Korematsu as he faced yet another civil rights battlefront. Another war, this one in the Middle East, and government action against suspects in the name of national security propelled the aging activist back into the arena. In 2003, at the age of eighty-four, Korematsu lent his name to an *amicus* brief filed with the U.S. Supreme Court on behalf of "enemy aliens" and citizens being held in Guantanamo Bay.

That case and others arose as a result of an order by President George W. Bush to imprison suspects in the nation's "war on terror." After terrorists attacked the World Trade Center in New York City and the Pentagon in 2001, Congress passed the Patriot Act, giving the president sweeping powers to fight terrorism. Bush claimed the act authorized him to jail suspected terrorists and interrogate them without allowing them access

Yaser Esam Hamdi, an American citizen born of Saudi parents, was imprisoned at Guantanamo Bay as an "enemy combatant" after his capture in Afghanistan in 2001. The Supreme Court ruled in 2004 that the U.S. government could not hold American citizens indefinitely without charges and a court hearing. Hamdi was later released and returned to Saudi Arabia, where he was raised.

to lawyers or court hearings. He also claimed that as "enemy combatants," the suspects were not covered by protections for prisoners outlined in the Geneva Conventions. The Bush administration seized foreigners and American citizens alike and denied them access to lawyers. By 2004, the government had issued formal charges against only five of the six hundred suspects held at the U.S. detention camp at the Guantanamo Bay naval base in Cuba.

The suspects challenged in court the administration's power to detain them without charges and a hearing. In the spring of 2004, the U.S. Supreme Court heard the cases of Yaser Esam Hamdi, an American citizen seized in Afghanistan, and a group of other suspects held in Guantanamo Bay. In arguing the cases, government lawyers argued that the Court did not have the authority or the expertise to "second-guess" the president's power to detain and question suspects.

This time the U.S. Supreme Court came down on the side of prisoners' rights. In an eight to one decision issued in June 2004, the Court ruled that Hamdi had the right to a court hearing on his detention. "A state of war," wrote Justice Sandra Day O'Connor in the Hamdi decision, "is not a blank check for the President when it comes to the rights of the nation's citizens." Justice Antonin Scalia, one of the most conservative members of the Court, reaffirmed the rights of the accused in a concurring opinion in the Hamdi case: "The very core of liberty secured by our Anglo-Saxon system of separated powers has been freedom from indefinite imprisonment at the will of the executive."

A second decision gave foreign suspects held in Guantanamo Bay the right to a hearing. Six of the nine justices agreed in the Guantanamo case that the government cannot continue to hold suspects indefinitely without charges and reviews by the court.

Following the Supreme Court decisions, the U.S. government released 150 prisoners and began military tribunals in 200 cases. Those were still in progress in early 2005. Charges were dropped against Army chaplain James Yee, Oregon attorney Brandon Mayfield, and computer science student Sami Omar Al-Hussayen, among others. Several others, including John Walker Lindh, a twenty-year-old California man captured in Afghanistan, were convicted and sentenced to jail terms.

In September 2004, the Justice Department announced it would release Hamdi without ever taking him to trial. After more than three years in custody, the young detainee returned to Saudi Arabia, where he was raised. Hamdi, the son of Saudi parents, was born in the United States. In a deal with the U.S. government, Hamdi agreed to give up his American citizenship in exchange for his freedom. He continues to hold Saudi citizenship. The *Hamdi* case raised questions of the legitimacy of the Pentagon's charges against other detainees.

Civil rights activists and advocates for the suspects hailed the *Hamdi* and Guantanamo Bay decisions. "At a minimum, [government officials] must now come forward with some evidence," said attorney Joseph Margulies. "You don't simply hold people in a lawless void based on nothing more than executive say-so."

Commenting on the Guantanamo Bay case, Korematsu looked back on his experiences of more than sixty years ago and the lessons they should have taught:

> I know what it is like to be at the other end of such scapegoating and how difficult it is to wipe away the unjustified suspicions once they are created. If someone is a spy or terrorist they should be prosecuted. But no one should ever be locked away simply because they share the same race, ethnicity, or religion as a spy or terrorist. If that principle was not learned from the internment of Japanese Americans, then these are very dangerous times for our democracy.

TIMELINE

December 7, 1941
Attack on Pearl Harbor, Hawaii.

December 8, 1941
United States declares war on Japan.

December 11, 1941
United States declares war on Germany.

February 19, 1942
President Franklin D. Roosevelt issues Executive Order No. 9066, allowing restricted military zones to be set up and authorizing "any or all persons" to be excluded from the zones.

February 20, 1942
Secretary Henry L. Stimson authorizes General John DeWitt to enforce Executive Order No. 9066.

March 2, 1942
General DeWitt issues Proclamation No. 1, which makes the western half of the West Coast states a restricted military zone.

March 18, 1942
President Roosevelt signs Executive Order No. 9102, setting up the War Relocation Authority.

March 21, 1942
Congress passes and Roosevelt signs Public Law 503 making it a crime to violate military orders given under Executive Order No. 9066.

March 24, 1942
Civilian Exclusion Order No. 1 orders evacuation of all Japanese
Americans from Bainbridge Island, Washington. First of more than
one hundred exclusion orders to force Japanese Americans from the
West Coast and into temporary assembly camps and then to perma-
nent internment camps.

March 27, 1942
Proclamation No. 4 bars Japanese Americans from moving from
western sections of the West Coast.

May 19, 1942
Civilian Restriction Order No. 1 forbids detainees from leaving
assembly camps.

May 30, 1942
Police arrest Fred Korematsu for violating the exclusion order as he
walks down the streets of San Leandro, California.

June 2, 1942
Proclamation No. 6 bars Japanese Americans from moving from
eastern sections of the West Coast.

November 3, 1942
Last of Japanese Americans moved to internment camps.

February 8, 1943
All detainees seventeen years old or older required to fill out loyalty
questionnaires.

June 21, 1943
U.S. Supreme Court rules in *Hirabayashi* v. *United States* and *Yasui* v.
United States that the curfew directed at Japanese Americans under
Executive Order 9066 is constitutional.

September 13, 1943
Tule Lake camp set up as a prison for Japanese-American detainees
considered "disloyal."

January 14, 1944
President Roosevelt announces that Nisei men will be drafted to serve
in the U.S. military.

December 17, 1944
U.S. Army announces that Japanese Americans will be allowed to return to the West Coast beginning January 2, 1945.

December 18, 1944
U.S. Supreme Court rules in *Korematsu* v. *United States* that the exclusion of Japanese Americans from the West Coast is constitutional. A second ruling, in *Ex parte Mitsuye Endo*, bars the U.S. government from holding loyal Japanese-American citizens in internment camps.

January 2, 1945
The exclusion of Japanese Americans from the West Coast is lifted. Some are allowed to return, but others continue to be held in camps.

May 7, 1945
Germany surrenders, ending the war in Europe.

August 6, 1945
U.S. forces drop an atomic bomb on Hiroshima.

August 9, 1945
United States drops second atomic bomb on Nagasaki.

August 14, 1945
Japan surrenders, ending the war in the Pacific.

March 20, 1946
Tule Lake, the last of the internment sites, closes.

July 15, 1946
The 442nd Regimental Combat Team of Nisei soldiers is honored at the White House as the most-decorated unit in the war.

June 16, 1983
The Commission on Wartime Relocation and Internment of Civilians issues report to Congress recommending reparations to former Japanese-American internees.

November 10, 1983
Federal Judge Marilyn Hall Patel overturns wartime conviction of Fred Korematsu and denounces the U.S. Supreme Court's decision in the *Korematsu* case.

August 10, 1988
Congress passes 1988 Civil Liberties Act authorizing payments of $20,000 and a presidential apology to every other former Japanese-American internee.

January 15, 1998
Fred Korematsu presented Medal of Freedom by President Bill Clinton.

June 28, 2004
U.S. Supreme Court rules detainees have the right to a hearing in *Yaser Hamdi* v. *Donald Rumsfeld* and *Shafiq Rasul et al.* v. *George W. Bush*. Korematsu had filed a brief in support of Hamdi's claims.

March 30, 2005
Fred Korematsu dies of a respiratory illness at his daughter's home in Larkspur, California. He was eighty-six.

NOTES

INTRODUCTION

p. 7, par. 1, *Ex parte Milligan*. 71 US 2 (1866).

p. 8, par. 2, *Korematsu v. United States*, 323 US 214 (1944), Justice Frank Murphy dissent.

p. 8, par. 5—p. 9, par. 1, p. 238.

p. 9, par. 2, *Adarand Constructors, Inc. v. Pena*, 515 U.S. 236 (1995).

p. 9, par. 3, *Korematsu v. United States*, 323 US 214 (1944), Jackson dissent.

p. 9, par. 4—p. 10, par. 2, William Rehnquist. *All the Laws but One*. New York: Vintage, 2000, pp. 68—69, 202—203.

CHAPTER 1

p. 12, par. 1, Fournier, Eric Paul. *Of Civil Wrongs and Rights: The Fred Korematsu Story*. New York: Public Broadcasting System, 2001. http://www.pbs.org/pov/pov2001/ofcivilwrongsandrights

p. 13, par. 3—p. 19, par. 1, The Asia Society. "Linking the Past to Present: Asian Americans Then and Now," 1996. http://www.askasia.org/frclasrm/readings/r000192.htm

p. 19, par. 2, American Memory. "Immigration." Library of Congress, 2004. http://memory.loc.gov/learn/features/immig/alt/japanese3.html

CHAPTER 2

p. 20, par. 1, United States Commission on Wartime Relocation and Internment of Civilians. *Personal Justice Denied: Report of the Commission on Wartime Relocation and Internment of Civilians*. Washington, DC: United States Commission on Wartime Relocation and Internment of Civilians, 1983, p. 5.

p. 20, par. 2—p. 21, par. 1, Eric Paul Fournier. *Of Civil Wrongs and Rights: The Fred Korematsu Story*. New York: Public Broadcasting System, 2001. http://www.pbs.org/pov/pov2001/ofcivilwrongsand rights

p. 21, par. 3, United States Commission on Wartime Relocation and Internment of Civilians. *Personal Justice Denied*, p. 284.

p. 22, par. 2, "First Japanese Ready to Leave Coast," *The San Francisco News*, March 19, 1942. Cited by the Museum of the City of San Francisco, www.sfmuseum.org/hist8/intern2.html

p. 22, par. 3—p. 23, par. 1, Lewis H. Carlson, and George A. Colburn. *In Their Place: White America Defines Her Minorities 1850—1950*. New York: John. Wiley and Sons, 1972, p. 243.
http://www.yale.edu/ynhti/curriculum/units/1982/3/82.03.01.x.html

p. 23, par. 3, Richard Lawrence Miller. "Confiscations from Japanese-Americans During World War II, 2001."
http://www.fear.org/RMillerJ—A.html

p. 23, par. 5, p. 27, par. 1, National Park Service. "The War Relocation Camps of World War II: When Fear was Stronger than Justice."
http://www.cr.nps.gov/nr/twhp/wwwlps/lessons/89manzanar/89 facts1.htm

p. 27, pars. 2—3, *Santa Cruz Sentinel—News*, December 18, 1941, p. 1.

p. 27, par. 4, W. H. Anderson. "The Question of Japanese-Americans," *Los Angeles Times*, Feb. 2, 1942.

p. 27, par. 5, *Santa Cruz Sentinel-News*, February 19, 1942, p. 1.

p. 28, pars. 1 and 2, La Mesa City Council Minutes, February 10, 1942. Cited in "The Internment of the Japanese of San Diego County During the Second World War," by Gerald Schlenker, *The Journal of San Diego History*, Spring 1972, vol. 18, no. 2,
http://www.sandiegohistory.org/journal/72winter/internment.htm

p. 28, par. 3, Walter Lippman. "The Fifth Column on the Coast," February 13, 1942. http://www.cr.nps.gov/nr/twhp/wwwlps/ lessons/89manzanar/89facets1.htm

p. 29, par. 4, p. 30, par. 1, Peter Irons. *Justice at War: The Story of the Japanese American Internment Cases*. New York: Oxford University Press, 1983, p. 360. From *In Brief Authority* by Francis Biddle. Garden City, NY: Doubleday, 1962, pp. 213 and 226.

p. 30, par. 2, United States Commission on Wartime Relocation and Internment of Citizens. *Personal Justice Denied*, p. 57. Citing the Roberts Commission Report.

p. 30, par. 3—p. 31, par. 1, Steve Mount. "The U.S. Constitution on Line." http://www.usconstitution.net/consttop_mlaw.html

p. 31, par. 2, United States Commission on Wartime Relocation and Internment of Citizens. *Personal Justice Denied*, p. 6.

p. 32, par. 2, U.S. Congress, House of Representatives. "National Defense Migration," House report 2124, p. 25. Cited in Schlenker.

p. 33, par. 1, *Los Angeles Times*. Cited in *No Ordinary Time* by Doris Kearns Goodwin, New York: Simon & Schuster, 1994, p. 297.

p. 34, par. 2, United States Commission on Wartime Relocation and Internment of Civilians. *Personal Justice Denied*, p. 55.

p. 34, par. 3, Biddle. *In Brief Authority*, p. 224. Cited in Schlenker.

p. 35, par. 1, Franklin D. Roosevelt. Executive Order No. 9066.

p. 35, par. 2, Doris Kearns Goodwin. *No Ordinary Time*. New York: Simon & Schuster, 1994, p. 323.

p. 39, par. 1, United States Commission on Wartime Relocation and Internment of Civilians. *Personal Justice Denied*, pp. 102–103.

p. 39, par. 3, Gerald Schlenker. "The Internment of the Japanese of San Diego County During the Second World War,"*The Journal of San Diego History*, Spring 1972, vol. 18, no. 2, http://www.sandiegohistory.org/journal/72winter/internment.htm

p. 40, par. 3, par. 5, Tolan Committee testimony. Cited in *Personal Justice Denied*, p. 96.

p. 40, par. 4, U.S. Congress, House, National Defense Migration, House report 1911, pp. 13, 31; p. p. 40, par. 4, U.S. Congress, House, National Defense Migration, House report 2124, pp. 48–58. Cited in Schlenker.

p. 41, par. 2, Frank Miyamoto. "The Seattle JACL and Its Role in Evacuation," p. 26, File 6.24, JERS., cited in *Conscience and the Constitution*, Public Broadcasting System. Hohokus, NJ: Transit Media, 2000. http://www.pbs.org/itvs/conscience

p. 41, pars. 3 and 4, Public Broadcasting System. *Conscience and the Constitution*. Hohokus, NJ: Transit Media, 2000. http://www.pbs.org/itvs/conscience

p. 42, pars. 3 and 4, Franklin D. Roosevelt. Executive Order No. 9102.

p. 42, par. 4, "First Japanese ready to leave Coast." *The San Francisco News*, March 19, 1942.

p. 46, par. 1, United States Commission on Wartime Relocation and Internment of Civilians. *Personal Justice Denied*, p. 153.

p. 46, par. 4–p. 47, par. 2, Ibid., p. 155.

p. 47, par. 3, National Park Service. "Confinement and Ethnicity: An Overview of World War II Japanese American Relocation Sites: Manzanar Relocation Center." http://www.cr.nps.gov/history/online_books/anthropology74/ce8a.htm

p. 48, pars. 2 and 3, Ibid.

p. 51, par. 3, Ibid.

p. 52, par. 2, Ibid..

CHAPTER 3

p. 54, par. 4—p. 55, par. 1, Peter Irons. *Justice at War: The Story of the Japanese American Internment Cases*. New York: Oxford University Press, 1983, p. 93.

p. 55, par. 3, Fred Korematsu. "Do We Really Need to Relearn the Lessons of Japanese American Internment?" *San Francisco Chronicle*, Open Forum, September 16, 2004.

p. 55, par. 4, David Margolick. "Legal Legend Urges Victims to Speak Out." *The New York Times*, Nov. 24, 1984, p. 25.

p. 56, pars. 1 and 2, Peter Irons. *Justice at War*, pp. 93, 96.

p. 56, par. 5—p. 57, par. 1, "Minoru Yasui." Human and Constitutional Rights Resource page, Columbia University Law School.
http://www.hrcr.org/ccr/yasui.html

p. 57, pars. 2 and 3, "45 Years Later, an Apology from the U.S. Government." *A&S Perspectives*, Newsletter of the University of Washington College of Arts and Sciences, Winter 2000.
www.artsci.washington.edu/newsletter/Winter00/Hirabayashi.htm

p. 58, par. 4—p. 59, par. 1, "Constitutional Amendment to Deny Citizenship to U.S. Born Japs Will Be Sought," UPI, *Watsonville Register—Pajaronian*, May 18, 1943, p. 3.
http://www.santacruzpl.org/history/ww2/9066/citizenship.shtm

p. 59, par. 2, Peter Irons. *Justice at War*, p. 152.

p. 60, par. 2, Irons, Ibid., pp. 152—154.

p. 60, par. 3, Peter Irons. *The Courage of Their Convictions: Sixteen Americans Who Fought Their Way to the Supreme Court*. New York: Penguin Books, 1990, pp. 50—62.

p. 62, par. 2, Peter Irons. *Justice at War*, p. 176.

p. 62, par. 4, *San Francisco Examiner*, February 20, 1943, p. 4, cited in Irons, p. 178.

p. 62, par. 6—p. 63, par. 1, Peter Irons. *Justice at War*, p. 178.

CHAPTER 4

p. 64, par. 2, Peter Irons. *Justice at War: The Story of the Japanese American Internment Cases*. New York: Oxford University Press, 1983, pp. 183—185.

p. 66, par. 1—p. 67, par. 1, Ibid., pp. 204—205.

p. 67, par. 4, p. 71, par. 1, Eric Paul Fournier. *Of Civil Wrongs and Rights: The Fred Korematsu Story*. New York: Public Broadcasting

System, 2001. http://www.pbs.org/pov/pov2001/ofcivilwrongsan
drights

p. 71, par. 4, Peter Irons. *Justice at War*, pp. 194–195.

p. 72, par. 2, Ibid., pp. 216–217.

p. 76, pars. 1 and 2, "Citizens Betrayed: The Hidden Story of Tule
Lake." Tule Lake Committee, 2002.
http://www.tulelake.org/2004–pilgrimage

p. 76, par. 3, George Takei. *To the Stars*. New York: Simon & Schuster, 1994.

p. 76, par. 4–p. 77, par. 1, United States Commission on Wartime
Relocation and Internment of Civilians. *Personal Justice Denied:
Report of the Commission on Wartime Relocation and Internment
of Civilians*. Washington, DC: United States Commission on
Wartime Relocation and Internment of Civilians, 1983, p. 192.

p. 77, par. 2, Irons. *Justice at War*, p. 201.

p. 77, par. 3, Burt Takeuchi, "Liberation of Dachau by Japanese
Americans," Nihonmachi Outreach Committee, San Jose,
California. http://asianguy.com/articles/dachau.html

p. 77, par. 4–p. 78, par. 3, United States Commission on Wartime
Relocation and Internment of Civilians. *Personal Justice Denied*,
pp. 203–204.

p. 80, par. 1, Ibid., p. 264.

p. 80, par. 3–p. 81, par. 1, Peter Irons. *Justice at War*, p. 220.

p. 82, par. 1, *Ex parte Milligan*, 7 U.S. 2 (1866)

p. 82, par. 3, Peter Irons. *Justice at War*, p. 220. (citing 1 U.S. Law
Week, 3344–47 (1943).

p. 83, par. 2–4, Ibid., p. 222.

p. 83, par. 5–p. 84, par. 1, Ibid., p. 223.

p. 84, par. 3, Ibid., p. 225.

p. 85, par. 3.

p. 86, par. 3–p. 87, par. 1, *McCleskey v. Zant*, 499 US 467 (1991),
quoting *Brown v. Allen*, 344 U.S. 443, 512 (1952), opinion of
Frankfurter, J.

p. 87, par. 1, *Harris v. Nelson*, 394 U.S. 286, 290–91 (1969).

p. 89, pars. 2 and 3, *Hirabayashi v. United States*, 320 US 81 (1943),
Chief Justice Harlan Stone majority opinion.

p. 89, par. 4, *Hirabayashi v. United States*, 320 US 81 (1943), Justice
William O. Douglas concurring opinion.

p. 89, par. 5, Roger Daniels. *Prisoners Without Trial*. New York: Hill
and Wang, 1993, p. 59.

p. 89, par. 5–90, par. 1, *Hirabayashi v. United States*, 320 US 81
(1943), Justice Frank Murphy concurring opinion.

p. 90, par. 4, *Hirabayashi* v. *United States*, 320 US 81 (1943), Justice Wiley B. Rutledge concurring opinion.

p. 91, par. 2, Peter Irons. *The Courage of Their Convictions: Sixteen Americans Who Fought Their Way to the Supreme Court*. New York: Penguin Books, 1990, pp. 50–62.

CHAPTER 5

p. 93, par. 3, Eric Paul Fournier. *Of Civil Wrongs and Rights: The Fred Korematsu Story*. New York: Public Broadcasting System, 2001. http://www.pbs.org/pov/pov2001/ofcivilwrongsandrights

p. 97, par. 3, *Korematsu* v. *United States*, 323 US 214 (1944), i, pp. 40–41.

p. 99, par. 2, *Korematsu* v. *United States*, pp. 18–58.

p. 99, par. 4–p. 100, par. 1, *Korematsu* v. *United States*, pp. 15–26.

p. 100, par. 2, Eric Paul Fournier. *Of Civil Wrongs and Rights*. http://www.pbs.org/pov/pov2001/ofcivilwrongsandrights

p. 100, par. 4–p. 101, par. 1, *Korematsu* v. *United States*, pp. 34–96. *Korematsu* v. *United States*, 323 US 214 (1944), p. 2.

p. 101, par. 2, brief of ACLU, *Korematsu* v. *United States*, p. 2.

p. 101, pars. 3 and 4, Ibid., p. 26.

p. 101, par. 5, Ibid.

p. 102, par. 3–p. 103, par. 4, Peter Irons. *Justice at War: The Story of the Japanese American Internment Cases*. New York: Oxford University Press, 1983, pp. 312–319.

CHAPTER 6

p. 104, par. 1, Lewis Wood. "Supreme Court Upholds Return of Loyal Japanese to West Coast." *The New York Times*, Dec. 19, 1944, p. 1.

p. 104, par. 4–p. 105, par. 1, *Korematsu* v. *United States*, 323 US 214 (1944).

p. 106, par. 1, Ibid.

p. 106, par. 2, *Korematsu* v. *United States*, 323 US 214 (1944), Justice Felix Frankfurter concurring opinion.

p. 106, par. 4–p. 107, par. 1, *Korematsu* v. *United States*, 323 US 214 (1944), Justice Owen Roberts dissent.

p. 107, par. 1, Ibid.

p. 107, par. 2–4, *Korematsu* v. *United States*, 323 US 214 (1944), Justice Frank Murphy dissent.

p. 109, pars. 1 and 2, Ibid.

p. 109, par. 3–p. 110, par. 2, *Korematsu* v. *United States*, 323 US 214 (1944), Justice Robert Jackson dissent.

p. 110, par. 3–p. 111, par. 1, Eric Paul Fournier. *Of Civil Wrongs and*

Rights: The Fred Korematsu Story. New York: Public Broadcasting System, 2001. http://www.pbs.org/pov/pov2001/ofcivilwrongsand rights

p. 111, par. 2, "Exiles' Return." *The New York Times,* December 22, 1944, p. 16.

p. 111, par. 3, Eric Paul Fournier. *Of Civil Wrongs and Rights.* http://www.pbs.org/pov/pov2001/ofcivilwrongsandrights.

p. 111, par. 6—p. 112, par. 1, *Ex parte Endo,* 323 US 283 (1944), Justice William O. Douglas majority opinion.

p. 112, par. 2, *Ex parte Endo,* 323 US 283 (1944), Justice Frank Murphy dissent.

p. 112, pars. 3 and 4, *Ex parte Endo,* 323 US 283 (1944), Justice Owen Roberts dissent.

p. 113, par. 1, "Ban on Japanese Lifted on Coast." *The New York Times,* Dec. 18, 1944, p. 1.

p. 113, par. 2, Congressional Record. 100th Cong. 2nd Sess., 134 Cong. Rec. Senate, 5412, May 10, 1988. May 10, 1988.

p. 113, par. 3, *Duncan* v. *Kahanamoku,* 327 US 304 (1946).

p. 113, par. 4—p. 114, par. 1, *Youngstown Co.* v. *Sawyer,* 343 U.S. 579 (1952).

p. 114, par. 2, *New York Times* v. *United States,* 403 U.S. 713 (1971).

p. 115, par. 2 p. 116, par. 1, Peter Irons. *Justice at War: The Story of the Japanese American Internment Cases.* New York: Oxford University Press, 1983, p. 204.

CHAPTER 7

p. 117, pars. 2 and 3, Eric Paul Fournier. *Of Civil Wrongs and Rights: The Fred Korematsu Story.* New York: Public Broadcasting System, 2001. http://www.pbs.org/pov/pov2001/ofcivilwrongsandrights

p. 118, par. 2, Ibid.

p. 119, par. 2, Ibid.

p. 119, par. 3—p. 120, par. 4, *Korematsu* v. *United States,* 584 F. Supp. 1406 (N.D. Cal. 1984). Cited in the *Congressional Record.*

p. 120, par. 5—p. 123, par. 1, "45 Years Later, an Apology from the U.S. Government." *A&S Perspectives,* Newsletter of the University of Washington College of Arts and Sciences, Winter 2000. www.artsci.washington.edu/ newsletter/Winter00/Hirabayashi.htm

p. 123, par. 4, p. 125, pars. 1–3, "Presidential Medal of Freedom Recipient Fred Toyosaburo." Medal of Freedom Web site, Korematsu. http://www.medaloffreedom.com/FredKorematsu.htm

p. 127, par. 3, Linda Greenhouse. "*The Supreme Court: Detainees; Access to Courts.*" *The New York Times,* June 29, 2004, p. 1.

p. 128, pars. 1 and 2, p. 127, par. 1, *Rasul, et al.,* v. *Bush*, et al., No. 03–334.

p. 128, par. 4, MSNBC staff. "Court: Terror Suspects Can Challenge Detentions." June 28, 2004. http://www.msnbc.msn.com/id/5316401

p. 129, pars. 1 and 2, Fred Korematsu. "Do We Really Need to Relearn the Lessons of Japanese American Internment?" *San Francisco Chronicle*, Open Forum, September 16, 2004.

All Web sites accessible as of June 15, 2005.

Further Information

BOOKS

Alonso, Karen. *Korematsu* v. *United States: Japanese-American Internment Camps* (Landmark Supreme Court Cases). Berkeley Heights, NJ: Enslow Publishers, 1998.

Chin, Steven A., and David Tamura. *When Justice Failed: The Fred Korematsu Story* (Stories of America). Austin, Texas: Steck-Vaughn, 1992.

Daniels, Roger. *Concentration Camps USA: Japanese Americans and World War II*. New York, Holt, Rinehart and Winston, 1971.

_____. *Prisoners Without Trial: Japanese Americans in World War II*. New York: Hill and Wang, 1993.

Girdner, Audrie, and Anne Loftis. *The Great Betrayal: The Evacuation of the Japanese-Americans During World War II*. New York: Macmillan, 1969.

Harth, Erica, ed. *Last Witnesses: Reflections on the Wartime Internment of Japanese Americans*. New York: Palgrave, 2001.

Houston, Jeanne Wakatsuki, and James D. Houston. *Farewell to Manzanar: A True Story of Japanese American Experience During and After the World War II Internment*. New York: Laurel Leaf, 1983.

Inada, Lawson Fusao. *Only What We Could Carry: The Japanese American Internment Experience*. Berkeley, CA: Heyday Books, 2000.

Irons, Peter. *Justice at War: The Story of the Japanese American Internment Cases*. New York: Oxford University Press, 1983.

_____. *War Powers: How the Imperial Presidency Hijacked the Constitution*. New York: Metropolitan Books, 2005.

Kikuchi, Charles. *The Kikuchi Diary: Chronicle From an American Concentration Camp: The Tanforan Journals of Charles Kikuchi*. Urbana. University of Illinois Press, 1973.

Levine, Ellen. *A Fence Away From Freedom: Japanese Americans and World War II*. New York: G. P. Putnam's, 1995.

Lowman, David D. *Magic: The Untold Story of U.S. Intelligence and the Evacuation of Japanese Residents from the West Coast during WW II*. Provo, UT: Athena Press, 2000.

Muller, Eric L. *Free to Die for Their Country: The Story of the Japanese American Draft Resisters in World War II* (Chicago Series in Law and Society. Chicago: University of Chicago Press, 2001.

Murray, Alice Yang. *What Did the Internment of Japanese Americans Mean?* (Historians at Work). New York: Bedford/St. Martin's, 2000.

Nishimoto, Richard S. (Richard Shigeaki). *Inside an American Concentration Camp: Japanese American Resistance at Poston, Arizona*. Tucson: University of Arizona Press, 1995.

Okubo, Miné. *Citizen 13660 /Drawings & text by Miné Okubo*. Seattle: University of Washington Press, 1983.

Robinson, Greg. *By Order of the President: FDR and the Internment of Japanese Americans*. Cambridge, MA: Harvard University Press, 2001.

Smith, Page. *Democracy on Trial: The Japanese American Evacuation and Relocation in World War II*. New York : Simon & Schuster, 1995.

Uchida, Yoshiko. *Desert Exile: The Uprooting of a Japanese-American Family*. Seattle: University of Washington Press, 2002.

United States Commission on Wartime Relocation and Internment of Civilians. *Personal Justice Denied: Report of the Commission on Wartime Relocation and Internment of Civilians*. The Civil Liberties Public Education Fund and University of Washington Press, 1997.

Weglyn, Michi. *Years of Infamy: The Untold Story of America's Concentration Camps*. Seattle: University of Washington Press, 1996.

VIDEOTAPES

Abe, Frank. *Conscience and the Constitution*. Hohokus, NJ: Transit Media, 2000. http://www.pbs.org/itvs/conscience

Foster, Rick. *Dust Storm: Art and Survival in a Time of Paranoia.* http://ducndcdrama.org/pCHT_DustStorm.htm

Fournier, Eric Paul. *Of Civil Wrongs and Rights: The Fred Korematsu Story*. New York: Public Broadcasting System, 2001. http://www.pbs.org/pov/pov2001/ofcivilwrongsandrights/

MGTV. *Defining Moments: Frank Murphy, Fred Korematsu, and the Internment of Japanese Americans During World War II*. Michigan Government Television, 1999.
http://www.mgtv.org/defining_moments.cfm

Omori, Emiko. *Rabbit in the Moon*. New York: Public Broadcasting System, 1999.
http://www.pbs.org/pov/pov1999/rabbitinthemoon/index.html

WEB SITES

Children of the Camps: Internment History. Public Broadcasting System, 2001
http://www.pbs.org/childofcamp/history

Confinement and Ethnicity: An Overview of World War II Japanese American Relocation Sites, National Park Service
http://www.cr.nps.gov/history/online_books/anthropology74/index.htm

FindLaw (U.S. Supreme Court cases)
http://www.findlaw.com/casecode/supreme.html

Geocities internment site and links to many related Web sites
http://www.geocities.com/Athens/8420/main.html

History Matters. American Social History Project/Center for Media & Learning, City University of New York, and the Center for History and New Media, George Mason University
http://historymatters.gmu.edu

Japanese American Exhibit and Access Project, University of Washington Libraries
http://www.lib.washington.edu/exhibits/harmony

Japanese American Internment Curriculum documents, San Francisco State University
http://bss.sfsu.edu/internment/documents.html

Japanese American Internment Experience
http://alterasian.com/internment

Japanese American Network links
http://www.janet.org/janet_history/ja_history.html

Korematsu v. *United States* (1944), U.S. Department of State.
http://usinfo.state.gov/usa/infousa/facts/democrac/65.htm

Legal Information Institute, Cornell Law School
http://www.law.cornell.edu

A More Perfect Union. Smithsonian Institute, National Museum of American History
http://americanhistory.si.edu/perfectunion/experience/index.html

NARA, U.S. National Archives & Records Administration
http://www.archives.gov

Oyez Project: U.S. Supreme Court Multimedia Web site
http://www.oyez.org/oyez/frontpage

Supreme Court Historical Society
http://www.supremecourthistory.org

Supreme Court of the United States site
http://www.supremecourtus.gov

Topaz: Japanese American WWII Internment Camp, Topaz Museum
http://topazmuseum.org/index.html

USS Arizona Preservation Project 2004, National Park Service
http://www.nps.gov/usar/index.htm

All Web sites accessible as of June 15, 2005.

BIBLIOGRAPHY

BOOKS

Carlson, Lewis H., and George A. Colburn. *In Their Place: White America Defines Her Minorities 1850–1950*. New York: John Wiley and Sons, 1972.

Daniels, Roger. *Prisoners Without Trial*. New York: Hill and Wang, 1993.

Goodwin, Doris Kearns. *No Ordinary Time*. New York: Simon & Schuster, 1994.

Irons, Peter. *The Courage of Their Convictions: Sixteen Americans Who Fought Their Way to the Supreme Court*. New York: Penguin Books, 1990.

_____. *Justice at War: The Story of the Japanese American Internment Cases*. New York: Oxford University Press, 1983.

Murray, Alice Yang. *What Did the Internment of Japanese Americans Mean?* (Historians at Work). New York: Bedford/St. Martin's, 2000.

Rehnquist, William. *All the Laws but One*. New York: Vintage, 2000.

Takei, George. *To the Stars*. New York: Simon & Schuster, 1994.

United States Commission on Wartime Relocation and Internment of Civilians. *Personal Justice Denied: Report of the Commission on Wartime Relocation and Internment of Civilians*. The Civil Liberties Public Education Fund and University of Washington Press 1997.

Weglyn, Michi. *Years of Infamy: The Untold Story of America's Concentration Camps*. Seattle: University of Washington Press, 1996.

AUDIO/VIDEO

Abe, Frank. *Conscience and the Constitution*, Public Broadcasting System. Hohokus, N.J.: Transit Media, 2000.

Edwards, Bob. "New Exhibit at the National Postal Museum in Washington, D.C.," *Morning Edition*, May 9, 2001.

Foster, Rick. *Dust Storm: Art and Survival in a Time of Paranoia*. http://duendedrama.org/pCHT_DustStorm.htm

Fournier, Eric Paul. *Of Civil Wrongs and Rights: The Fred Korematsu Story*. New York: Public Broadcasting System, 2001. http://www.pbs.org/pov/pov2001/ofcivilwrongsandrights

MGTV. *Defining Moments: Frank Murphy, Fred Korematsu, and the Internment of Japanese Americans During World War II*. Michigan Government Television, 1999. http://www.mgtv.org/defining_moments.cfm

Omori, Emiko. *Rabbit in the Moon*. New York: Public Broadcasting System, 1999. http://www.pbs.org/pov/pov1999/rabbitinthemoon/index.html

WEB SITES

Administrative Office of the U.S. Courts. http://www.uscourts.gov

American Italian Historical Association, Western Regional Chapter, "Luna Storia Segreta." http://www.io.com/~segreta/during/internment.html

American Memory, Library of Congress. http://memory.loc.gov

The Asia Society. http://www.askasia.org/frclasrm/readings/r000192.htm

Avalon Project at Yale Law School, Documents in Law, History and Diplomacy. http://www.yale.edu/lawweb/avalon/avalon.htm

FindLaw, U.S. Supreme Court decisions.
http://www.findlaw.com/casecode/supreme.html

Human and Constitutional Rights Resource page, Columbia
University Law School.
http://www.hrcr.org/ccr/yasui.html

Iowa Court Information System.
http://www.judicial.state.ia.us/students/6/

Legal Information Institute, Cornell Law School.
www.law.cornell.edu/constitution/constitution.billofrights.html

The Library of Congress, American Memory site.
http://memory.loc.gov/ammem

Library of Congress's Thomas: Legislative Information on the Internet.
http://thomas.loc.gov

Medal of Freedom.
http://www.medaloffreedom.com/FredKorematsu.htm

National Asian American Telecommunications Association.
http://www.jainternment.org/postwar/ongoing.html

National Park Service.
http://www.cr.nps.gov

Nihonmachi Outreach Committee, San Jose, California.
http://asianguy.com/articles/dachau.html

Oyez, U.S. Supreme Court Multimedia site.
http://www.oyez.org/oyez/frontpage

School of Law, Emory, Macmillan Law Library. Amendments to the
Constitution.
http://www.law.emory.edu/FEDERAL/usconst/amend.html

Tule Lake Committee, 2002.
http://www.tulelake.org/2004-pilgrimage

U.S. Constitution Online.
http://www.usconstitution.net

U. S. Department of Justice, "Redress for Internment."
http://www.usdoj.gov/crt/ora/main.html

U.S. Government Printing Office.
http://www.gpoaccess.gov/constitution/browse.html

U.S. National Archives & Records Administration, Federal Register.
http://www.archives.gov

U.S. Supreme Court Historical Society.
http://www.supremecourthistory.org

U.S. Supreme Court of the United States site.
http://www.supremecourtus.gov

The Virtual Museum of the City of San Francisco, "Internment of San Francisco Japanese."
http://www.sfmuseum.net/war/evactxt.html

All Web sites accessible as of June 15, 2005.

ARTICLES

Anderson, W. H. "The Question of Japanese-Americans," *Los Angeles Times*, February 2, 1942.

"Ban on Japanese Lifted on Coast," *The New York Times*, December 18, 1944, p. 1.

"Exiles' Return," *The New York Times*, December 22, 1944, p. 16.

"First Japanese Ready to Leave Coast," *The San Francisco News*, March 19, 1942.

"45 Years Later, an Apology from the U.S. Government," *A&S Perspectives*, Newsletter of the University of Washington College of Arts and Sciences, Winter 2000.

Greenhouse, Linda. "The Supreme Court: Detainees; Access to Courts," *The New York Times*, June 29, 2004, p. 1.

Korematsu, Fred. "Do We Really Need to Relearn the Lessons of Japanese American Internment?" *San Francisco Chronicle*, Open Forum, September 16, 2004.

Margolick, David. "Legal Legend Urges Victims to Speak Out," *The New York Times*, November 24, 1984.

Miller, Richard Lawrence. "Confiscations from Japanese-Americans During World War II, 2001." http://www.fear.org/RMillerJ-A.html

MSNBC staff. "Court: Terror suspects can challenge detentions." June 28, 2004.

"Relocation of Japanese-Americans," War Relocation Authority publication, May 1943.

Schlenker, Gerald. "The Internment of the Japanese of San Diego County During the Second World War," *The Journal of San Diego History*, Spring 1972, vol. 18, no. 2.

United Press International. "Constitutional Amendment to Deny Citizenship to U.S. Born Japs Will Be Sought," *Watsonville Register-Pajaronian*, May 18, 1943.

Wood, Lewis. "Supreme Court Upholds Return of Loyal Japanese to West Coast," *The New York Times*, December 19, 1944, p. 1.

STATUTES, COURT CASES, DOCUMENTS

Civilian Exclusion Order No. 1

Civilian Exclusion Order No. 34

Congressional Record. 100th Cong. 2nd Sess., 134 Cong. Rec. Senate, 5412, May 10, 1988. May 10, 1988.

DeWitt, General J. L. *Final Report: Japanese Evacuation From the West Coast 1942*, Washington, D.C.: Government Printing Office, 1943.

Executive Order 9066: Japanese Relocation Order (1942).

Executive Order No. 9102 (1942).

Instructions to All Persons of Japanese Ancestry, April 1, 1942.

La Mesa City Council Minutes, February 10, 1942.

Proclamation No. 1, March 2, 1942.

Public Law 503.

U.S. Congress, House, "National Defense Migration," House report 2124.

U.S. Congress, House, Tolan Committee testimony and report.

U.S. Constitution, Articles 1-10 (Bill of Rights).

COURT CASES

Adarand Constructors, Inc. v. Pena, 515 U.S. 236 (1995).

Brown v. Allen, 344 U.S. 443 (1952).

Duncan v. Kahanamoku, 327 US 304 (1946).

Ex parte Endo, 323 US 283 (1944).

Ex parte Milligan, 71 US 2 (1866).

Hamdi v. Rumsfeld et. al., 124 US 2633 (2004).

Harris v. Nelson, 394 U.S. 286, 290 91 (1969).

Hirabayashi v. United States, 320 US 81 (1943).

Hirabayashi v. United States, 627 F. Supp. 1445 (W.D. Wash. 1986).

Korematsu v. United States, 323 US 214 (1944).

Korematsu v. United States, 584 F. Supp. 1406 (N.D. Cal. 1984).

McCleskey v. Zant, 499 US 467 (1991).

Odah, et al., v. United States et al., No. 03-343.

Jose Padilla v. Commander C.T. Hanft, USN (District of South Carolina — Case No. 2:04-2221-26AJ), 2004.

Rasul, et al., v. Bush, et al., No. 03-334.

Donald Rumsfeld v. Jose Padilla (United States Supreme Court—Case

No. 03-1027), 2004.

Yasui v. *United States*, 320 US 115 (1943).

Yasui v. *United States*, 83-151 BE (D. Or. 1984), remanded, 772 F.2d 1496 (9th Cir. 1985).

Youngstown Co. v. *Sawyer*, 343 U.S. 579 (1952).

Index

about the author

SUSAN DUDLEY GOLD has written more than three dozen books for middle-school and high-school students on a variety of topics, including American history, health issues, law, and space. Her most recent works for Marshall Cavendish Benchmark are *Gun Control* in the Open for Debate series, and *Roe v. Wade: A Woman's Choice?*, *Brown v. Board of Education: Separate but Equal?*, and *The Pentagon Papers: National Security or the Right to Know*—all in the Supreme Court Milestones series. She is currently working on four more books about Supreme Court cases.

Gold has also written several books on Maine history. Among her many careers in journalism are stints as a reporter for a daily newspaper, managing editor of two statewide business magazines, and freelance writer for several regional publications. She and her husband, John Gold, own and operate a Web design and publishing business. Susan has received numerous awards for her writing and design work. Susan and her husband, also a children's book author, live in Maine. They have one son, Samuel.